Finance for IT Managers Simplified

SRIBATSA DAS, MBA

ISBN-10: 1499730144
ISBN-13: 978-1499730142

DEDICATION

To wife, Chaitali, who supported through my Business School and always believed that I could do anything creative and innovative.

CONTENTS

ACKNOWLEDGMENTS

I acknowledge the insightful teachings of the Professors at New York University's Leonard N. Stern School of Business who not only provided me deep understanding of finance but also inspired me to launch entrepreneurial venture. I spent countless hours in writing this book that kept me away from my elementary school children's activities. I acknowledge their sacrifice and support throughout the writing process.

1 INTRODUCTION

Cost is a critical component of IT projects. For projects to commence, business case needs to be prepared, submitted and approved to secure funding. Once a project is implemented, system needs to be maintained. Depending on the phase of the project, cost needs to be capitalized or expensed. Maintenance cost needs to be expensed. Categorizing cost as capital or operating expense impacts the firm's bottom-line; therefore, must be carried out meticulously according to the prevailing accounting standards. To make decisions before starting a project or making a decision whether to continue with a project mid-way, managers often face situations to make "what if" decisions. Net Present Value, Internal Rate of Return and Payback period play a role in making such decisions. Since servers and off the shelf commercial software cost large sum of money to purchase and then to maintain, Total Cost of Ownership is a way to measure the life time cost to own the product. Often leasing equipment becomes an available option. Managers need to be able to compare financing vs. leasing. Many vendors propose equipment of unequal life. To compare the cost, Estimated Annual Cost is used. Similar to Estimated Annual Cost, Estimated Monthly Cost can be computed. In IT, a shared service is an acceptable concept. Once shared services are built, projects or applications need to be charged to recover the expense. Chargeback model is explained as well. In the end, detailed business cases are presented. Reader can utilize the examples to prepare own business case. This book aims at covering finance concepts as they apply to IT functions so that IT Managers and Project Managers can manage project or departmental finance effectively.

Chapter 2 – Time Value of Money – This chapter covers interest rate, present value (PV), Future Value (FV), Net Present Value (NPV) and Payment. It explains how NPV is used for deciding IT Projects.

Chapter 3 – Internal Rate of Return (IRR) – This chapter explains IRR. It presents several examples of IRR. It presents how IRR is used for deciding IT projects as well as the limitations of IRR.

Chapter 4 – Opportunity Cost – This chapter explains the economic value of the best alternative given up by making a decision.

Chapter 5 – Sunk Cost – This chapter explains how the money spent does not impact future decision on a project.

Chapter 6 – Cost of Capital – This chapter explains the concept behind cost of capital and how to calculate one. This rate is used for discounting cash flows for IT projects.

Chapter 7 – Payback Period – This chapter explains the payback period is. It presents a detail example of payback period.

Chapter 8 – Expected Value (EV) – This chapter describes what EV is and presents examples to calculate EV of a project based on different outcome.

Chapter 9 – Expected Annual Cost (EAC) – This chapter presents how to compare machines of unequal lives.

Chapter 10 – Capital vs. Operating Expense – This chapter explains what these are. It presents IT costs and categorizes them into Capital vs. Operating Expense. SDLC Waterfall and Agile methodology are presented and a phase within each life cycle is categorized into Capital vs. Operating Expense. Purchase of package software, customization of package software, software development, equipment purchase and maintenance cost are categorized into Capital vs. Operating Expense with plenty of examples.

Chapter 11 – Depreciation and Amortization – This chapter explains how hardware is depreciated while software and goodwill are amortized with examples.

Chapter 12 – Total Cost of Ownership (TCO) – This chapter explains what the concept behind TCO is. It presents TCO for a server, a web site, an ERP system, a Data Warehouse System and a mobile app.

Chapter 13 – Chargeback – This chapter explains how to develop a chargeback model. It presents examples of chargeback model for a Load Testing CoE, Incident Management System and Private Cloud.

Chapter 14 – Financing vs. Leasing – This chapter explains the concepts behind financing and leasing. It presents examples to explain the concepts.

Chapter 15 – Cost Benefit Analysis (CBA) – This chapter explains the concepts behind cost benefit analysis. It presents examples to explain the concepts. It explains how NPV and IRR play a role in deciding a project from among multiple competing projects.

Chapter 16 – Off-Shoring and Outsourcing – This chapter explains the concepts. It presents various scenarios to understand costs associated with off shoring and out-sourcing.

Chapter 17 – Business Case – This chapter presents how to develop a business case. It presents a mobile app project and the sales volume and income statement. In the end, the analysis calculates IRR from the cash flow.

Hypothetical examples are presented to explain the concepts clearly.

Numbers used in the examples are fictitious. Every project is unique. The cost and revenue drivers need to be carefully identified and analyzed. However, the concepts are important and are applicable to IT divisions of many companies.

Drawing cash flow diagrams makes the cash flows easier to understand. According to commonly used practice in finance, an up arrow represents cash inflow and cash outflow is presented by down arrow on cash flow diagrams. This book follows the same convention.

2 TIME VALUE OF MONEY

Time is money, why? Due to inflation, the value of money depreciates. However, if money is invested at a rate of return exceeding inflation, then investment appreciates. Investor expects return on investment due to the risk associated with the investment. Risk arises from inflation risk, credit risk, interest rate risk and currency risk as well as country risk. Because of risk, lenders charge interest rate to borrowers. This chapter introduces the concepts of time value of money – interest rate, present value (PV), future value (FV) and net present value (NPV). NPV is the most important financial indicator to decide whether to pursue a project. If NPV is positive, then, the project should be selected. If multiple projects are under consideration, the project with the highest NPV should be selected.

Interest rate is a quantifiable measure of risk associated with a cash flow. A portion of interest rate reflects inflation. The portion reflects credit risk. When a consumer borrows money from a bank to purchase car, bank charges interest on the borrowed money to get compensated for the investment risk. The higher the risk, the higher the interest rate is demanded by the lenders. Interest rate of secured loans such as auto loan and home loan is lower than unsecured loan such as credit card debt. Treasury bills, notes, bonds are free from default risk; hence the rate on these is called risk free rate. However, they are not free from market risk.

Present Value (PV) of a future cash flow is the value of the cash flow today adjusted by the risk associated with the cash flow. Interest rate is a quantifiable measure of risk associated with a cash flow. If the future value is FV, time is t years and interest rate is r. Let's assume that interest is compounded annually. Then, the present value of future cash flow today is $PV = FV \div (1+r)^t$.

Example 2-1: A start-up promised Business Compass LLC to pay

4

$50,000 after 5 years for 5% interest rate compounding annually for investment made today. How much would Business Compass LLC needs to invest provided the company is willing to take the risk of investing with the start-up?

PV of FV $50,000 is $50,000÷$(1+5÷100)^5$= $39,176.30

Example 2-2: A start-up promised Business Compass® LLC to pay $50,000 after 5 years for 5% interest rate compounding monthly for investment made today. How much would Business Compass LLC needs to invest provided the company is willing to take the risk of investing with the start-up?

Rate per period = 5%÷12
Number of periods = 5 years × 12 months/year = 60

PV of FV $50,000 is $50,000÷$(1+5÷1200)^{60}$= $38,960.26

Example 2-3: A start-up promised Business Compass® LLC to pay $50,000 after 5 years for 5% interest rate compounding weekly for investment made today. How much would Business Compass® LLC needs to invest provided the company is willing to take the risk of investing with the start-up?

Rate per period = 5%÷52
Number of periods = 5 years × 52 months/year = 260
PV of FV $50,000 is $50,000÷$(1+5÷5200)^{260}$= $38,944.71

Example 2-4: A start-up promised Business Compass® LLC to pay $50,000 after 5 years for 5% interest rate compounding daily for investment made today. How much would Business Compass® LLC needs to invest provided the company is willing to take the risk of investing with the start-up?

Rate per period = 5%÷365
Number of periods = 5 years × 365 days/year = 1825
PV of FV $50,000 is $50,000÷$(1+5÷36500)^{1825}$= $38,940.70

Example 2-5: A start-up promised Business Compass® LLC to pay $50,000 after 5 years for 5% interest rate compounding continuously for investment made today. How much would Business Compass® LLC needs to invest provided the company is willing to take the risk of investing with the start-up?

$PV = FV \times e^{-rt}$.

PV of FV \$50,000 is \$50,000$\times e^{-5\% \times 5} =$ \$50,000$\times e^{-0.25} =$ \$50,000 $\times$ 0.778800783 = \$38,940.03

Future Value (FV) of a cash flow is the risk adjusted return at the end of the investment period. If the present value of the investment is PV, the interest rate is r, investment time is t and interest compounds annually, Future Value $FV = PV \times (1+r)^t$.

Example 2-6: Business Compass® LLC decided to invest in \$50,000 a certified deposit in the local bank for 5 years at 5% interest rate compounding annually. At the end of the 5th year, Business Compass® LLC will receive \$63,814.

$FV = \$50,000 \times (1+5 \div 100)^5 = \$63,814$

Example 2-7: Business Compass® LLC decided to invest in \$50,000 a certified deposit in the local bank for 5 years at 5% interest rate compounding monthly. At the end of the 5th year, Business Compass® LLC will receive \$64,167

Rate per period = $5\% \div 12$
Number of periods = $5 \times 12 = 60$

$FV = \$50,000 \times (1+5 \div 1200)^{60} = \$64,167$

Example 2-8: Business Compass® LLC decided to invest in \$50,000 a certified deposit in the local bank for 5 years at 5% interest rate compounding weekly. At the end of the 5th year, Business Compass® LLC will receive \$64,167

Rate per period = $5\% \div 52$
Number of periods = 5 years $\times$ 52 weeks/year = 260

$FV = \$50,000 \times (1+5 \div 5200)^{260} = \$64,193$

Example 2-9: Business Compass LLC decided to invest in \$50,000 a certified deposit in the local bank for 5 years at 5% interest rate compounding daily. At the end of the 5th year, Business Compass® LLC will receive \$64,167

Rate per period = $5\% \div 365$
Number of periods = 5 years $\times$ 365 days/year = 1825

$FV = \$50,000 \times (1+5\div5200)^{1825} = \$64,200$

Example 2-10: Business Compass® LLC decided to invest in $50,000 a certified deposit in the local bank for 5 years at 5% interest rate compounding continuously. At the end of the 5th year, Business Compass® LLC will receive $64,167

$FV = PV \times e^{rt}$.

$FV = \$50,000 \times e^{5\% \times 5} = \$50,000 \times e^{0.05 \times 5} = \$50,000 \times e^{0.25}$
$= \$50,000 \times 1.284 = \$64,201$

Net Present Value (NPV) of a series of cash flows is the sum of present values of the series of future cash flows $(CF_0 \ldots CF_n)$ discounted by a given discount rate of interest rate.

$$NPV = \sum_{t=0..n} CF_t \div (1+r)^t$$

Example 2.11 – Business Compass® LLC invested $3,000,000 to launch a new mobile app called MBA Sidekick to enable MBA Students and professionals to perform finance, statistics, economics, strategy and operational related analysis using mobile devices. At the end of the first year, the start-up is expected to receive revenue of $500,000. At the end of second year, the revenue is expected to be $1,500,000. At the end of the third year, the expected incremental revenue is $2,000,000. Interest rate at which Business Compass® LLC can borrow is 10%. What is the NPV of the cash flows?

Present Value (PV) of Cash Flow now is -$3,000,000 due to the investment
PV of cash flow received at the end of the first years is   PV($500,000 @ 10%) = $454,545.45
NPV after receiving first year revenue is -$3,000,000+$454,545.45 = ($2,545,454.55)

PV of cash flow received at the end of the second years is   PV($1,500,000 @ 10%) = $1,239,669
NPV after receiving first second revenue is -$3,000,000+$454,545.45+ $1,239,669= -$1,305,785

PV of cash flow received at the end of the third years is   PV($2,000,000 @ 10%) = $1,502,629
NPV after receiving third year revenue is -$3,000,000+$454,545.45+ $1,239,669 + $1,502,629 = $196,844.48

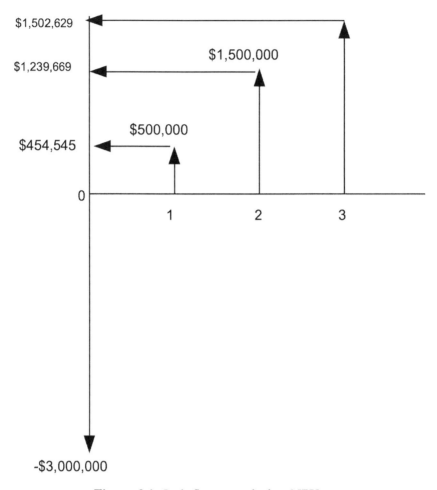

Figure 2.1: Cash flows to calculate NPV

Cash flow convention uses down arrow to represent cash outflow and up arrow to represent cash inflow.

NPV is the most important financial parameter of a project used in deciding whether to pursue the project. If the NPV of a project is positive then the project should be considered, else needs to be rejected. When multiple projects are considered, then the project with the highest NPV is the winner.

In example 2.11, the NPV of the project is positive, hence should be pursued.

Example 2.12: Business Compass® LLC is considering investing in two projects to create mobile apps MBA Sidekick and Mobile Statistics Professor®. The initial investment and revenue earned is shown in the table below. Let's assume that Business Compass® LLC will borrow the money at 10% interest. Which project should Business Compass® LLC pursue?

Project	Initial Investment	Year					NPV
		1	2	3	4	5	
MBA Sidekick	3	2	2	2	2	2	5.7
Mobile Statistics Professor	2	3	3	3	3	3	11.06

Table 2.1: Cash flow of two investments. All numbers are shown in $ million. Interest rate is 10%.

NPV of Mobile Statistics Professor® is higher than that of MBA Sidekick project. Therefore, Mobile Statistics Professor® project should be pursued.

Example 2.13: Business Compass® LLC is considering load testing (also known as performance testing) of its ERP/ERM system. It can purchase 30-day virtual user generator licenses or perpetual virtual user generator licenses to simulate system load. System needs to be able to perform well with 500 users logged on to the system simultaneously. Each 30-day virtual user generator license costs $25. Each perpetual license costs $500. The system has a need to continue load testing once a month for 3 years. Let's assume that Business Compass® LLC will borrow the money at 10% interest. Which licensing option is a better choice for Business Compass® LLC pursue?

Cost of 500 30-day virtual user generator license = 500 × $25 = $12,500
Cost of 500 perpetual virtual user generator licenses = 500 × 5800 = $250,000

NPV of monthly payment in the amount $15,000 for 30-day license for 3 years or 36 months at discount rate 10% ÷ 12 per month = Σ $12,500 × $(1+10\% \div 12)^{-t}$ where t=1 to 36 = $387,390.44

NPV of 500 perpetual virtual user generator licenses $250,000

Purchasing 500 perpetual virtual user generator license will cost less; therefore, is an economically superior option than purchasing monthly 30-day virtual user licenses.

		Year	

Project	Initial Investment	1	2	3	4	5	NPV
MBA Sidekick	3	2	2	2	2	2	5.7
Mobile Statistics Professor	2	3	3	3	3	3	11.06

Table 2.2: Cash flow of two investments. All numbers are shown in $ million. Interest rate is 10%.

NPV of Mobile Statistics Professor is higher than that of MBA Sidekick project. Therefore, Mobile Statistics Professor project should be pursued.

Payment of a loan for a period t at interest rate r per period is a follows. PMT = Principal or PV $\times$ [r $\div$ {1-(1+r)$^{-t}$}].

PMT is available as a function in major spreadsheets and financial calculator.

Example 2.13 – Business Compass® LLC borrowed $40,000 at 5% APR for 5 years to purchase a shuttle van for transportation of its employees between Morristown, New Jersey and Mahwah, New Jersey. How much will Business Compass pay per month towards loan payment?

Interest rate is 5% APR.
Interest rate per month is 5% $\div$ 12=0.416%
Time is 5 years $\times$ 12 months/year=60 months

r = 0.416%, t = 60, Principal = $40,000

PMT = $40,000 $\times$ [0.416%$\div$ {1-(1+0.416%)$^{-60}$}]= $40,000 $\times$ [0.416%$\div$ {1-(1.00416)$^{-60}$}]= $40,000 $\times$ [0.416%$\div$ 1-0.7795]= $40,000 $\times$ [0.00416$\div$ 0.2207]=$40,000 $\times$ 0.01887=$754.84

Example 2.14 – Business Compass® LLC borrowed $40,000 to purchase a mid-range computer at 5% APR for 5 years to host a new web site. This equipment will be installed in its headquarters in Randolph, NJ. It has to pay 10% down payment. Sales Tax rate is 7%. How much will Business Compass® LLC pay per month towards loan payment?

Interest rate is 5% APR.
Interest rate per month is 5% $\div$ 12=0.416%

Time is 5 years × 12 months/year=60 months

$r = 0.416\%$, $t = 60$, Principal $= \$40,000$

Amount financed = Equipment Purchase Price + Sales Tax - Down payment = $\$40,000 + \$40,000 \times 7\%$ - $\$40,000 \times 10\%$ = $\$40,000 + \$2,800$ - $\$4,000 = \$38,800$

PMT = $\$38,800 \times [0.416\% \div \{1-(1+0.416\%)^{-60}\}]$= $\$38,800 \times [0.416\% \div \{1-(1.00416)^{-60}\}]$= $\$38,800 \times [0.416\% \div 1-0.7795]$= $\$38,800 \times [0.00416 \div 0.2207]$=$\$38,800 \times 0.01887$=$\$732.20$

Some payments are made at the beginning of the period while others are paid at the end of the period. Insurance payment is made in advance. Mortgage payments are made at the end of the month. Hosting payments are made at the end of the month. Utility bills are paid at the end of the month. Computer hardware and software support fee, which is typically 15% of the purchase cost, is paid in advance.

3 INTERNAL RATE OF RETURN

Internal Rate of Return (IRR) is the discount rate at which the Net Present Value (NPV) of a series of cash flows equates to 0. IRR is intended to measure average expected annual rate of return of a project. However, IRR has its drawbacks – projects of different scale can return the same IRR, multiple IRRs if cash flow sign changes and the rule is reversed for lending vs. borrowing. Sometimes, a cash follow may not yield an IRR. IRR of a project is also the return on investment (ROI) of a project. IRR needs to be higher than the cost of capital to select a project. IRR is the second best measure after NPV to decide whether to pursue a project.

Example 3.1 – Business Compass® LLC invested $3,000,000 to launch a new mobile app called MBA Sidekick to enable MBA Students and professionals to perform finance, statistics, economics, strategy and operational related analysis using mobile devices. At the end of the first year, the start-up is expected to receive revenue of $500,000. At the end of second year, the revenue is expected to be $1,500,000. At the end of the third year, the expected incremental revenue is $2,000,000.

Let's assume that the discount rate is $r\%$.

Present Value (PV) of Cash Flow now is -$3,000,000 due to the investment

PV of cash flow received at the end of the first years is $\frac{\$500,000}{(1+r)} = \$500,000 \times (1+r)^{-1}$

PV of cash flow received at the end of the second years is $\$1,500,000 \times (1+r)^{-2}$

PV of cash flow received at the end of the third years is $\$2,000,000 \times (1+r)^{-3}$

NPV of 4 cash flows is

-$3,000,000 +

$500,000 $\times (1+r)^{-1}+$

$1,500,000 \times (1+r)^{-2}+$
$2,000,000 \times (1+r)^{-3}$

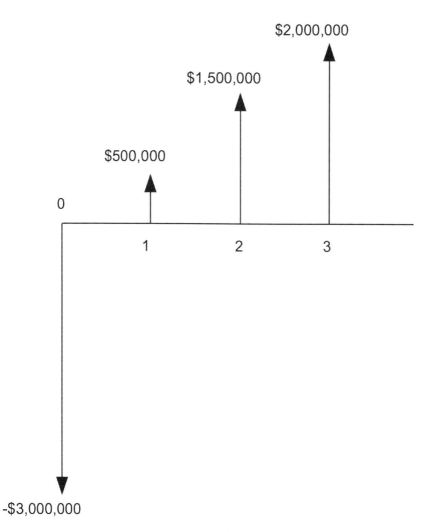

Figure 3-1: Cash Flows

To calculate IRR, equate NPV to 0.

$-\$3,000,000 + \$500,000 \times (1+r)^{-1} + \$1,500,000 \times (1+r)^{-2} + \$2,000,000 \times (1+r)^{-3}$
$= 0$

The NPV equation is a polynomial. The root of the polynomial is IRR.

When equation is solved, the root of the equation is 13%. So, r is 13%. In other words, the IRR of the 4 series cash flow is 13%.

How is IRR Calculated?

Calculating IRR involves solving the polynomial. This can be carried out iteratively by guessing values, but can be time consuming. Newton-Raphson and Runge-Kutta methods are typically to solve the root of polynomials. Fortunately, IRR is available as a function in spreadsheets as well as in Financial Calculators.

Is it possible to calculate IRR all the times?

If the sign of cash flow changes sign more than once, then the polynomial may result in multiple roots. Sometimes, the polynomial cannot solve.

Now, let's consider another example. This example is similar to Example 3.1 except the numbers are $1/10^{th}$ of the numbers used in Example 3.1.

Example 3.2 – Business Compass® LLC invested $300,000 to launch a new mobile app called MBA Sidekick to enable MBA Students and professionals to perform finance, statistics, economics, strategy and operational related analysis using mobile devices. At the end of the first year, the start-up is expected to receive revenue of $50,000. At the end of second year, the revenue is expected to be $150,000. At the end of the third year, the expected incremental revenue is $200,000.

Let's assume that the discount rate is r%.

Present Value (PV) of Cash Flow now is -$300,000 due to the investment
PV of cash flow received at the end of the first years is $50,000 \times (1+r)^{-1}$
PV of cash flow received at the end of the second years is $150,000 \times (1+r)^{-2}$
PV of cash flow received at the end of the third years is $200,000 \times (1+r)^{-3}$
NPV of 4 cash flows is $-\$300,000 + \$50,000 \times (1+r)^{-1} + \$150,000 \times (1+r)^{-2} + \$200,000 \times (1+r)^{-3}$

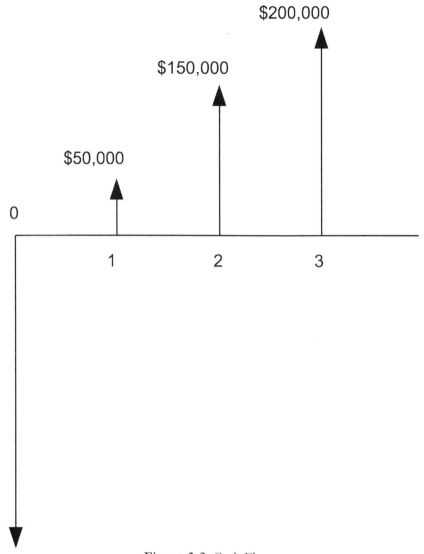

Figure 3-2: Cash Flows

To calculate IRR, equate NPV to 0.

-$300,000 + $50,000 $\times$ (1+r)$^{-1}$ $^+$ $150,000$\times$(1+r)$^{-2}$
+$200,000 $\times$ (1+r)$^{-3}$ =0

The NPV equation is a polynomial. The root of the polynomial is IRR.

When equation is solved, the root of the equation is 13%. So, r is 13%. In other words, the IRR of the 4 series cash flow is 13%.

Example 3.1 and 3.2 demonstrate that IRR for the cash flows of different scale can be the same. This is a drawback of use of IRR to decide which project to select.

Now, let's consider a cash flow reflecting multiple investments or where cash flow changes sign more than once.

Example 3.3 – Business Compass® LLC invested $500,000 to launch a new mobile app called MBA Sidekick to enable MBA Students and professionals to perform finance, statistics, economics, strategy and operational related analysis using mobile devices. At the end of the first year, the start-up is expected to receive revenue of $5,000,000. At the end of second year, the Business Compass® LLC is expected to expand MBA Sidekick into multiple mobile platforms and geographies where multiple language and devices need to be supported. This is expected to result in a net investment of $5,000,000 in the second year. Revenue is expected to be flat over the next three years due to further investment.

Let's assume that the discount rate is $r\%$.

Present Value (PV) of Cash Flow now is -$500,000 due to the investment
PV of cash flow received at the end of the first years is $5,000,000 \times (1+r)^{-1}$
PV of cash flow received at the end of the second years is -$5,000,000 \times (1+r)^{-2}$
PV of cash flow from 3rd, 4th and 5th year is 0.
NPV of 6 cash flows is -$500,000 + $5,000,000 \times (1+r)^{-1}$ -$5,000,000 \times (1+r)^{-2}$

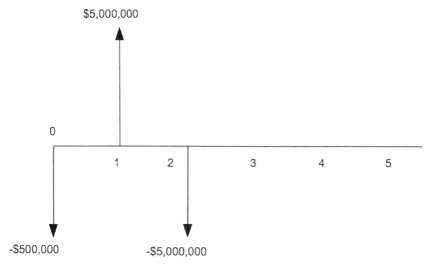

Figure 3-3: Cash Flows

To calculate IRR, equate NPV to 0.

$-\$500,000 + \$5,000,000 \times (1+r)^{-1} - \$5,000,000 \times (1+r)^{-2} = 0$

The NPV equation is a polynomial. The root of the polynomial is IRR.

When equation is solved, two roots emerge – 13% and 787%. So, which IRR to choose to make project approval decision? This is the second drawback of IRR.

How to use IRR to decide whether to pursue a project?

If the IRR of the project is greater than the cost of capital, then select the project.

Lending versus borrowing

When lending, rate of return needs to be higher than IRR of the project
When borrowing rate of return needs to be lower than IRR of the project

How to select a project from two projects with the same IRR?

Select the project with higher NPV.

Return on Investment or ROI of a project is the IRR of the project. ROI is commonly used term to understand whether management wants to commit resources to a project. ROI needs to be higher than the cost of the capital, for a project to be profitable.

To summarize, IRR is the next best measure to evaluate projects although IRR suffers from drawbacks related to scale, multiple roots, and reversal of rules between borrowing and lending as well as not converting to a solution in certain cash flows.

4 OPPORTUNITY COST

The value of the best alternative given up by making another choice. When multiple choices are presented, the opportunity cost of selecting a choice needs to be estimated to be sure that the correct decision is made.

Example 4.1: As a graduate student the founder of Business Compass® LLC has three options to earn money during summer. (a) work in a local fast food chain and earn $4.25 per hour minimum wage, (b) work as a research assistant and earn $10 per hour and in addition receive 25% off on tuition fee for classes taken during summer, (c) work as a teaching assistant and earn $9 per hour and in addition receive 50% off on tuition fee for classes taken during summer. Let's assume that the tuition fee for summer before the discount is $500 per credit hour up to 9 credit hours. Student can work 40 hours per week in summer. Student decided to pursue with option (c). Student enrolled in classes worth 9 credit hours while working full 40 hours. What is the opportunity cost?

Let's compute the economical value of each option.

Option (a): $4.25 per hour× 40 hours/week = $170
Option (b): $10 per hour× 40 hours/week + 9 credit hours × $500 per credit hour × 25%= $1,525
Option (c): $9 per hour× 40 hours/week + 9 credit hours × $500 per credit hour × 50%= $2,610
Option (c) offers the best value.
If the student were to choose option (a), opportunity cost would have been $2,610 - $170 = $2,440.
If the student were to choose option (b), opportunity cost would have been $2,610 - $1,525 = $1,085.

Example 4.2: The CTO of Business Compass® LLC has three choices to host altmanzscoreplus.com web site. The choices are (a) to purchase required hardware and software and host the web site internally which would cost $10,000 annually, (b) host the web site at a cloud service provider in the United States which would cost $9,900 annually, (c) host the web site in a foreign data center through a hosting provider which would cost $5,000. Let's assume that the site is critical to generating revenue for Business Compass LLC. The site gathers personally identifiable information (PII) and processes credit card. The website needs to offer high availability and fast response time to users. The CTO decided to proceed with option (a). Further assume that the vendor in option (b) and (c) are able to offer solutions at par with option (a) to mitigate PII and other privacy and security requirements. What is the opportunity cost?

The best solution will cost $5000, yet the one chosen costs $10,000. So, the opportunity cost is $10,000-$5,000=$5,000. The CTO forgoes $5,000 by not selecting option (c).

Example 4.3: The CTO of Business Compass® LLC has three projects to increase revenue. The choices are (a) to create a web service to provide Altman Z-Score+ corporate credit data to financial firms which will generate $10,000,000 over next 3 years, (b) to build a mobile app that will generate $5,000,000 revenue on average for next 3 years and (c) to build a desktop application to predict the stock market which will generate $6,000,000 revenue per year. Let's assume that the cost to build these three systems is comparable. The CTO decided to proceed with option (a). What is the opportunity cost?

Economic value of options a, b and c over 3 years is $10,000,000, $15,000,000 and $18,000,000. Option (a) is selected where as option (c) offers the greatest economic value. Therefore, the opportunity cost to Business Compass LLC due to the selection of option (a) is $18,000,000 - $10,000,000 = $8,000,000.

5 SUNK COST

Sunk cost of a project is the money that is spent already. Money already spent cannot be recovered. Therefore, the money spent is called sunk cost. Sunk cost is irrelevant to making

Example 5.1: Business Compass® LLC spent $3 million in building a mobile trading platform for traders over the past 3 years. In the mean time, a large international stock exchange has released its own mobile trading product. The stock exchange has started spending a lot of money in marketing the product. Business Compass® LLC's management is considering whether to so launch its product. Let's assume that it would cost another $2 million for Business Compass® LLC to be able to complete the product and to be able to launch the product. What consideration should be given to the 3 years and $3 million spent already?

Management needs to ignore the money and time spent since that time and money cannot be recovered. Decision to invest additional $2 million and time depends on the return Business Compass® LLC will receive from the investment.

Yes, time and money spent invoke a lot of emotions, but from an economic view point, these are irrelevant.

6 COST OF CAPITAL

Cost of Capital -A company raises capital by borrowing (or issuing debt) and by selling shares (or issuing equity). For the projects carried out by the company, cost of capital instead of cost of borrowing needs to be used for discounting cash flows generated by the internal projects. For IT projects, interest rate used for discounting cash flow is also called **cost of capital** or Weighted Average Cost of Capital (**WACC**) or **hurdle rate**. Cost of capital is the weighted average cost of after tax cost of debt and cost of equity weighted by their relative contribution to total capital.

Cost of Equity is Re
Cost of Debt if Rd
Tax Rate is T
Book Value of Debt is D
Market Value of Equity is E
Total Capital is D+E

Contribution of Debt to Total Capital is $\frac{D}{D+E}$

Contribution of Equity to Total Capital is $\frac{E}{D+E}$

$$\text{WACC} = \frac{Rd \times (1-T) \times D + Re \times E}{D+E}$$

Cost of Debt is the rate at which the company can borrow from a creditor. Determining cost of equity is much more involved and requires understanding the concepts of corporate finance to select a list of comparable companies, un-levering equity beta to arrive at average asset beta, then re-levering asset beta to arrive at the firm's equity beta, then applying Capital Asset Pricing Model (CAPM) to arrive at the equity beta of the firm. Therefore, it is much simpler to consult the finance or accounting partner associated with the project for the hurdle rate.

Example 6.1: Business Compass® LLC raised $30 million by issuing shares and $10 million by borrowing from lenders. Corporate tax rate for Business Compass LLC is 35%. Cost of debt is 7%. Cost of Equity is 9%. What is the hurdle rate for IT Projects?

D=$10 million
E = $30 million
T = 35%
Rd = 7%
Re = 9%

$$\text{WACC} = \frac{Rd \times (1-T) \times D + Re \times E}{D+E} = \frac{7\% \times (1-35\%) \times 10 + 9\% \times 30}{10+30} = \frac{7 \times 0.65 \times 10 + 9 \times 30}{40} = 7.89\%$$

Example 6.2: Levered up by raising debt and reducing equity sale. Business Compass® LLC raised $20 million by issuing shares and $20 million by borrowing from lenders. In this case, debt is raised and equity is reduced. Corporate tax rate for Business Compass® LLC is 35%. Cost of debt is 7%. Cost of Equity is 9%. What is the hurdle rate for IT Projects?

D=$20 million
E = $20 million
T = 35%
Rd = 7%
Re = 9%

$$\text{WACC} = \frac{Rd \times (1-T) \times D + Re \times E}{D+E} = \frac{7\% \times (1-35\%) \times 20 + 9\% \times 20}{10+30} = \frac{7 \times 0.65 \times 20 + 9 \times 20}{40} = 6.77\%$$

Example 6.3: All Equity Financed. Since Business Compass® LLC is a start-up, it finds difficult to raise capital by issuing debt. Therefore, it raised $50 million by issuing shares. Corporate tax rate for Business Compass® LLC is 35%. Cost of debt is 7%. Cost of Equity is 9%. What is the hurdle rate for IT Projects?

D=0
E = $50 million
T = 35%
Rd = 7%
Re = 9%

$$\text{WACC} = \frac{Rd \times (1-T) \times D + Re \times E}{D+E} = \frac{7\% \times (1-35\%) \times 0 + 9\% \times 50}{50} = 9\%$$

Example 6.4: All Debt Financed. Business Compass LLC has a stable cash flow. Therefore, it raised $50 million by issuing debt. Corporate tax rate for Business Compass® LLC is 35%. Cost of debt is 7%. Cost of Equity is 9%. What is the hurdle rate for IT Projects?

D=$50 million
E =0
T = 35%
Rd = 7%
Re = 9%

$$\text{WACC} = \frac{Rd \times (1-T) \times D + Re \times E}{D+E} = \frac{7\% \times (1-35\%) \times 50 + 9\% \times 0}{50} = 4.55\%$$

7 PAYBACK PERIOD

Payback Period is the amount of time it takes a project to recover the initial investment. This indicates the least amount of time capital will be tied up to break-even.

Example 7.1 – Business Compass® LLC invested $3,000,000 to launch a new mobile app called MBA Sidekick to enable MBA Students and professionals to perform finance, statistics, economics, strategy and operational related analysis using mobile devices. At the end of the first year, the start-up is expected to receive revenue of $500,000. At the end of second year, the revenue is expected to be $1,500,000. At the end of the third year, the expected incremental revenue is $2,000,000. Interest rate at which Business Compass® LLC can borrow is 10%.

Present Value (PV) of Cash Flow now is -$3,000,000 due to the investment
PV of cash flow received at the end of the first years is PV($500,000 @ 10%) = $454,545.45
NPV after receiving first year revenue is -$3,000,000+$454,545.45 = ($2,545,454.55)

PV of cash flow received at the end of the second years is PV($1,500,000 @ 10%) = $1,239,669
NPV after receiving first second revenue is -$3,000,000+$454,545.45+ $1,239,669= -$1,305,785

PV of cash flow received at the end of the third years is PV($2,000,000 @ 10%) = $1,502,629
NPV after receiving third year revenue is -$3,000,000+$454,545.45+ $1,239,669 + $1,502,629 = $196,844.48

In case the payback period is between 2 and 3 years. Since the monthly revenue is not known, conservative payback period is 3 years. Payback period is a buzzword used to determine project viability, but it is not. NPV and then IRR are better predictors of the project's economic superiority. Payback period impacts psychologically, and is imprinted into the minds of management, but is used less frequently.

In case the payback period is between 2 and 3 years. Since the monthly revenue is not known, conservative payback period is 3 years. Payback period is a buzzword used to determine project viability, but it is not. NPV and then IRR are better predictors of the project's economic superiority. Payback period impacts psychologically, and is imprinted into the minds of management, but is used less frequently.

8 EXPECTED VALUE

Expected value of an outcome is the weighted average value of the possible outcomes. Often IT projects are undertaken to increase units, revenue, call and close rate. While such projects are undertaken, depending upon the internal and external environment, the revenue generated can be high, medium or low. The expected value of the project will be the weighted average of values associated with each outcome. V_i and P_i are value and probability associated with each outcome. Expected value is the sum of the cross product of all V_i and P_i pairs.

$$E(V) = \Sigma \ V_i \times P_i$$

Example 8.1 – Business Compass® LLC invested $3,000,000 to launch a new mobile app called MBA Sidekick to enable MBA Students and professionals to perform finance, statistics, economics, strategy and operational related analysis using mobile devices. Management expects the Life Time Value of revenue generated from the mobile app as follows.

Product Reception	Probability	Value
Highly Successful	30%	$10,000,000
Moderately successful	60%	$7,000,000
Too bad, thus suffered total loss	10%	-$3,000,000

$E(V) = 30\% \times \$10,000,000 + 60\% \times \$7,000,000 - 10\% \times \$3,000,000 = \$6,900,000$

9 ESTIMATED ANNUAL COST

While making purchasing decisions, often a choice needs to be made from multiple options involving unequal asset life and maintenance cost. The initial purchase cost and subsequent maintenance cost can be annualized similar to mortgage payment. This is called effective annual cost (EAC). The option with the lowest EAC wins. If monthly cost needs to be compared, then Estimated Monthly Cost can be calculated. Comparing monthly vendor hosting fee with in-house hosting will require converting the in-house hosting fee to Estimated Monthly Cost.

Example 9.1: Business Compass® LLC is presented with two mid-range computer options to meet its growing demand for computing. The interest rate at which Business Compass® LLC can borrow from the local bank is 10%. All the numbers are in $ million. Table below presents the initial outlay and the annual maintenance cost. Which option to select?

Option	Initial Investment	Maintenance Cost			NPV	EAC
		Year 1	Year 2	Year 3		
1	10	2.5	2.5	2.5	16.2	$5.496
2	15	0.5	1	1	16.1	$5.366

Table 9.1: Investment and maintenance cost of 2 options

First of all, the NPV of each cash outflow. Next, NPV is converted to an annual payment or EAC. In this case, option 2 has a lower EAC compared to option 1. Therefore, option 2 is economically superior to option 1.

In IT, managers are often presented with the option of hosting infrastructure on premise vs. purchasing hosting from a service provide for a monthly fee. EAC is an effective way to make an economic decision.

Example 9.2 A 4 CPU 16GB RAM Linux server costs $2000 to purchase. The cost of rent is $20 per month. Maintenance cost is $10 per month. The cost of electricity consumed per month is $5. The life of the server is 3 years.

Alternately, virtual server with similar configuration is available from a hosting provider for $100 per month.

Let's assume that the borrowing cost is 10% per annum or 10% ÷ 12 per month.

The operating cost for owning the server is $20 + $10 + 5 = $35 per month. This recurring cost will be incurred throughout the life of the server that is 3 years or 36 months. The cash flows (which all negative) are shown in diagram below. The NPV of the cash flows is $3042.93. At 10% annual interest rate, the monthly payment (similar to EAC) is $130.45

Figure 9.1: Cash Flows for EAC

$2000 +Σ$35 ÷ (1+10%÷12)$^{-t}$ where t = 1 to 36
= $2000 +$1042.93 =$3042.93

Monthly payment of amount $3042.93 at 10% ÷ 12 monthly interest for 26 months or 3 years is $130.45.

In this case, the hosting cost is $100 while the cost of owning and operating per month is $130.42. Therefore, the option to host is economically superior.

10 CAPITAL VS. OPERATING EXPENSE

Capital expense is an expenditure incurred to create a future asset or a future benefit. This is often called capital expenditure or CapEx. Purchasing a new computer, buying a disk-array, building a new data center are some of the examples of CapEx.

Tangible assets; such as, hardware are depreciated over the life of the asset. Internal Revenue System's Modified Accelerated Deprecation (MACRS) treats life of Information system as 6 years under ADS system and 5 years under GDS system.

Intangible assets; such as intellectual property, good will (excess purchase price) are amortized over the life of the asset.

Operating expense is an expenditure incurred in ordinary course of business or to operate the business. Fee paid for software or hardware maintenance falls into operating expense. Salary paid to employees or contractors is considered as OpEx.

Operating Expense impacts income since expense needs to be deducted from revenue to arrive at income. CapEx needs to be depreciated or amortized depending on the type of the asset over the asset's life. Depreciation or amortization is reduced from the revenue to arrive at income. CapEx impacts income gradually whereas OpEx impacts income in the same reporting period. Every expense cannot be Capital Expense unless the nature of the expense fits the definition. There is a tendency in IT community to CapEx as much as possible where as the accounting groups working with IT typically ensures that the correct expense classification has been carried out.

FASB Financial Accounting Standards Number 86 spells out the criteria for accounting software development cost.

1. Treat cost as R&D expense until Technical Feasibility is reached
2. Technical Feasibility is reached until a detailed design is created or a working model is developed.

Accounting Standards until a company has established technical feasibility of software, the expense incurred towards R&D needs to be treated as operating expense.

Software can be developed for internal use or to be sold externally. In either case, the costs associated with the preliminary stages are R&D expense or operating expense until technical feasibility is established. The cost associated with stages of software development after the technical feasibility is established can be capitalized. Once the software is deployed internally, the support cost is operating expense. Bug fixes are operating expense. Feature enhancements can be capitalized.

Srl. No.	Category	CapEx	OpEx
1	Purchase of Software	✓	
2	Building new software	✓	✓
3	Purchasing Hardware	✓	
4	Purchasing Cloud Hosting		✓
5	Building software to convert data	✓	✓
6	Building Interface	✓	✓
7	Building Web Service	✓	✓
8	Building Software As a Service (SaaS) capability	✓	✓
9	Purchasing SaaS		✓
10	Customization to SaaS		✓
11	Purchasing Platform As a Service (PaaS)		✓
12	Building Platform As a Service (PaaS)	✓	✓
13	Purchasing Infrastructure as a Service (IaaS)		✓
14	Building Infrastructure as a Service (IaaS)	✓	✓
15	Travel unless part of		✓

Srl. No.	Category	CapEx	OpEx
	capital project		
16	Training		✓
17	Software Upgrade (except when they are made to SaaS, or the ones not increasing life of the software)		✓
18	Enhancement (except when they are made to SaaS, or the ones not increasing life of the software)	✓	
19	Maintenance		✓
20	Bug fix		✓
21	Applying patches		✓
22	Outsourcing maintenance & support		✓
23	Salaries paid (Capital Portion of project is capitalizable and operating expense portion is not capitalizable)	✓	✓

Table 10.1: Categorizing IT cost into OpEx vs. CapEx

Data Conversion - While building IT systems, often data needs to be converted from old system to new system or interfaces need to be developed to transfer data between systems. In general, Data conversion is an OpEx item since no value is created due to data conversion. Interfaces to transfer data between systems or APIs to transfer data from a source system to one or more targets are capitalized.

Srl. No.	Category	CapEx	OpEx
1	Converting old data to new system	✓	
2	Data Cleansing		✓
3	Data Archival		✓
4	Data Purging		✓
5	Data Reconciliation		✓

Table 10.2: Categorizing Data Conversion cost into OpEx vs. CapEx

IT Projects follow waterfall Software Development Life Cycle (SDLC) or

Agile SDLC where product is released progressively. Water fall SDLC follows feasibility assessment, analysis, design, development, testing, go-live and post-production support phases. Feasibility assessment, analysis, post-production supports are considered as operating expense. The rest of the phases are considered as capital expense.

Srl. No.	Category	CapEx	OpEx
1	Due diligence		✓
2	Analysis		✓
3	Functional Design		✓
4	Technical Design	✓	
5	Development	✓	
6	Testing	✓	
7	Deployment	✓	
8	Post production support		✓

Table 10.3: Categorizing IT cost of water fall SDLC into OpEx vs. CapEx

Building an Interface - While building IT systems, often data needs to be transferred between systems. Web Service is a new form of such interface. While building specific interface between two systems or building generic Web Service to be used by many down stream applications, depending on the phase of SDLC, the portion of the cost is either treated as operating expense or capital expense. Cost associated with Feasibility Study, Analysis and Post-Production support are treated as operating expense and the rest are treated as capital expense.

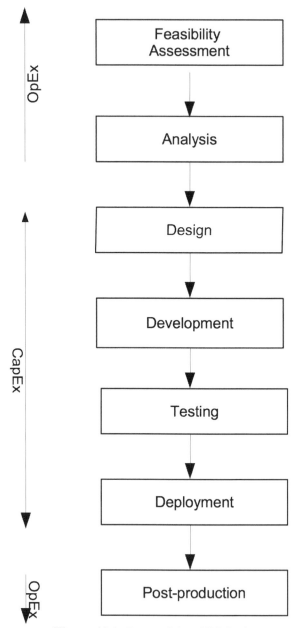

Figure 10.1: Categorizing SDLC phases to CapEx vs. OpEx

Example 10.1: Business Compass® LLC decided to create a new Data Warehousing system. Let's review the costs associated with various phases of the project and categorize the expense associated.

Srl. No.	Category	Cost	CapEx	OpEx

Srl. No.	Category	Cost	CapEx	OpEx
1	Studied feasibility	$150,000	✓	
2	Purchased mid-range servers	$3,000,000	✓	✓
3	Purchased ETL Software	$600,000	✓	
4	Purchased Analytics Software	$900,000	✓	
5	Purchased Data Cleansing Software	$1,000,000	✓	
6	Purchased National Change of Address and House-holding data for business	$50,000 per month	✓	
7	Purchased National Change of Address and House-holding data for households	$50,000 per month	✓	
58	Created logical design	$100,000	✓	
9	Created physical design	$10,000	✓	
10	Developed the system	$2,000,000	✓	
12	Tested the system	$200,000	✓	
13	Performed data conversion	$100,000	✓	
14	Trained users	$50,000		✓
15	Deployed the system	$100,000	✓	
16	Paid a vendor to perform system maintenance	$50,000 per month		✓
17	Enhanced system capability by launching mobile analytics	$100,000	✓	
18	Upgraded Operating System Software and	$150,000	✓	

Srl. No.	Category	Cost	CapEx	OpEx
	Database software version			
19	Traveled to Boston, San Diego and Denver during feasibility study	$50,000		✓
20	Traveled to Boston, San Diego and Denver design, development and testing phases	$150,000	✓	

Table 10.4: Categorizing IT cost of building a system into OpEx vs. CapEx

Now, let's consider Agile development methodology. The product is progressively elaborated. Initial few iterations are spent in creating a working model. Subsequent iterations enhance product functionality. The cost associated with the initial iterations until the feasibly is established, the cost associated with the creation of the product is treated as operating expense. The work performed after establishing feasibility is treated as capital expense.

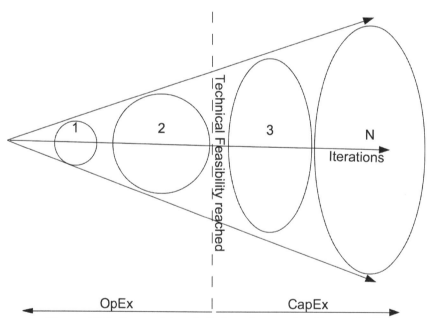

Figure 10.2: Categorizing Agile iterations to CapEx vs. OpEx

Example 10.2: Business Compass® LLC decided to create a new Mobile

App called Mobile Statistics Professor® using Agile methodology. Let's review the costs associated with software development and categorize them appropriately.

Srl. No.	Iteration	Functionality	Cost	CapEx	OpEx
1	0	Prototype	$50,000		✓
2	1	Added regression	$10,000	✓	
3	2	Added calculator	$10,000	✓	
4	3	Added data file upload and processing	$10,000	✓	
5	4	Added pretty graphics and charts	$10,000	✓	
6	5	Added print capability	$10,000	✓	
7	6	Added capability to send result as an email	$10,000	✓	

Table 10.5: Categorizing IT cost of Agile iterations into OpEx vs. CapEx

Project Management Life Cycle differs from Product Management Life Cycle such as Water Fall SDLC or Agile methodology life cycle. Project Management life cycle consist of initiation, planning, execution, control and closing. Cost associated with initiation and planning is typically OpEx while the rest are CapEx.

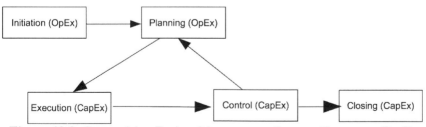

Figure 10.3: Categorizing Project Management Process Groups to CapEx vs. OpEx

11 DEPRECIATION AND AMORTIZATION

Tangible asset is depreciated due to wear and tear over the life of the asset. Intangible asset is amortized since the intellectual property becomes less valuable over time.

There are two types of depreciation – one from accounting point of view (or GAAP – Generally Accepted Accounting Principles) point of view and another from tax point of view (or IRS MACRS). GAAP follows straight-line depreciation where the value of the asset is spread over its useful life. Tax depreciation in USA follows MACRS (or Modified Accelerated Depreciation System) where the asset depreciates at a faster rate in the initial years and slowly in the later years. IRS Publication 946 explains how to depreciate property. For the IT purpose, the discussion will limit to GAAP depreciation and use straight-line depreciation of the asset.

Hardware; such as, Data Center, Computer Equipment, Servers, Telephone Equipment are depreciated. These have 5-year useful life. Typically, IRS GDS method is used for tax accounting.

Software is amortized. The life of the software is 3 years provided software is used without modification; such as; Commercial Off The Shelf (COTS) Software. If software is custom built or modified, then the life is 5 years.

Examples 11.1 – A computer is purchased for $3,000. It has a useful life of 5 years.

Year	GAAP Rate	GAAP Depreciation
1	20%	$600
2	20%	$600
3	20%	$600
4	20%	$600
5	20%	$600

Table 11.1: GAAP Depreciation of a computer

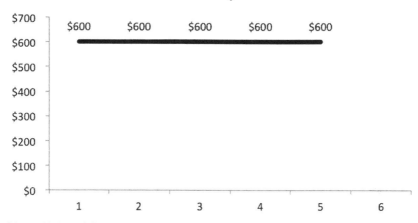

Chart 11.1: GAAP Depreciation of a computer

Examples 11.2 – Business Compass® LLC invested in a new CRM software. To deploy the software efficiently, the management decide to use the software "as is" without making any custom changes. Software is purchased. According MACRS GDS method, the has a useful life of 3 years for COTS. The purchase price of the software is $3 million.

Year	GAAP Rate	GAAP Depreciation
1	33.33%	$1 million
2	33.33	$1 million
3	33.33%	$1 million

Table 11.2: GAAP amortization of software

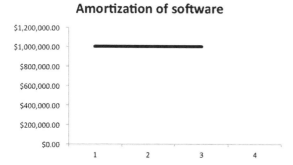

Chart 11.2: GAAP vs. MACRS Depreciation of a software

12 TOTAL COST OF OWNERSHIP

Total cost of ownership (TCO) of an asset (hardware or software) is the direct and indirect cost associated with owning and operating the asset during the life of the asset. TCO consists of the following

• Original purchase price of the computer hardware and software
• Incremental cost of hardware and software upgrades
• On-going monthly maintenance cost
• Cost of Technical support
• Cost of Change Management including Training

Example 12.1: Server purchased and to be running 24x7 for 5 years Business Compass LLC purchased a Linux Server to host its web site. The server needs to be running 24x7. The life of the server is 5 years. The server uses 50-Watt electricity on average. Electricity costs $0.45/kWh Assume that the borrowing cost to Business Compass® LLC is 10% per annum. Further assume that electricity cost remains the same for the life of the asset and there are no other costs.

For simplicity, monthly costs are converted to annual cost and then, NPV is calculated. For finer granularity, APR can be converted to monthly interest rate by diving 12 and NPV can be calculated using monthly interest rate and monthly cost.

Hourly power consumption - 50 Watts /1000 = 0.05 kWh
Daily power consummation = 24 × 0.05 kWh = 1.2 kWh
Yearly power consumption = 365 × 1.2 kWh= 438 kWh
Annual cost of power consumption = $0.45 per KWh x 438 kWh =$197.1
Assuming that the power cost to remain the same over the next 5 years, each year, $197.10 will be spent in running the server.

Year	Cost category	Cost
0	Initial investment	$3,000
1	Utility cost	$197.10
2	Utility cost	$197.10
3	Utility cost	$197.10
4	Utility cost	$197.10
5	Utility cost	$197.10

Table 12.1: Expenses associated with a server

NPV of the 6 cash flows or TCO = $3000 + Σ $197.10 $\times$ $(1+10\%)^{-t}$
where t = 1 to 5
= $3,000 + $747.50
=$3,747.50

The server purchase cost can be capitalized over 5 years and will be depreciated over 5 years. Utility cost will be treated as operating expense.

Example 12.2: Server purchased and to be running 24x7. Server maintenance performed. Now, let's expand example 8.1 and consider more realistic operating expenses. Business Compass® LLC purchased a Linux Server to host its web site. The server needs to be running 24x7. The life of the server is 5 years. The server uses 50-Watt electricity on average. Electricity costs $0.45/kWh Assume that the borrowing cost to Business Compass LLC is 10% per annum. Further assume that electricity cost increases 10% every year. The rack space is hosted in a data center that charges $20 rental fee per month. The server needs to be backed up once a week that costs $5 for backup. Maintenance patches and other upgrades are free for the life of the asset and there are no other costs.

For simplicity, monthly costs are converted to annual cost and then, NPV is calculated. For finer granularity, APR can be converted to monthly interest rate by diving 12 and NPV can be calculated using monthly interest rate and monthly cost.

From example 12.1, $197.10 will be spent in running the server the first year.
Rental cost per annum is $20 per month $\times$ 12 months = $240 per year
Backup cost per year = $5 $\times$ 52 weeks = $260 per year

Operating cost = Utility cost + Rental Cost + Backup Cost

First year operating cost = $197.10 + $240 + $260 = $697.10

Year	Cost category	Cost
0	Initial investment	$3000
1	Operating cost	$697.10
2	Operating cost	$716.81
3	Operating cost	$738.49
4	Operating cost	$762.34
5	Operating cost	$788.57

Table 12.2: Expenses associated with a server running 24x7

NPV of the 6 cash flows or TCO = $5,264.82

The server purchase cost can be capitalized over 5 years. Remaining portion of the initial investment will be treated as operating expense. Yearly operating cost will be treated as operating expense.

Example 12.3: Server is used to host a web site. Now, let's expand example 8.2 and consider that the server is used to host a web site. Business Compass® LLC purchased a Linux Server to host its web site. The server needs to be running 24x7. The life of the server is 5 years. The server uses 50-Watt electricity on average. Electricity costs $0.45/kWh Assume that the borrowing cost to Business Compass® LLC is 10% per annum. Further assume that electricity cost increases 10% every year. The rack space is hosted in a data center that charges $20 rental fee per month. The server needs to be backed up once a week that costs $5 for backup. Server maintenance patches and other upgrades cost $50 on average per year for the life of the asset.

Linux-Apache-MySQL-PHP (LAMP) stack is used for hosting the web site. The web-site domain name is financeforitmanagegerssimplified.com. It costs $15.99 to purchase and renew the domain each year. The web site needs to be virus scanned daily. $4.99 is spent monthly to scan virus. Since the web site processes payment, the site needs a SSL certificate that costs $69.99 per year. SSL needs to be purchased at the beginning of the year.

The cost to develop the web site is $5,000. Each month $500 is spent in maintenance and enhancement of the web site.

For simplicity, monthly costs are converted to annual cost and then, NPV is calculated. For finer granularity, APR can be converted to monthly interest rate by diving 12 and NPV can be calculated using monthly interest rate and monthly cost.

From example 12.1, \$197.10 will be spent in running the server the first year.

Rental cost per annum is \$20 per month × 12 months = \$240 per year
Backup cost per year = \$5 × 52 weeks = \$260 per year
Maintenance patches and upgrades = \$50 per year
Virus Scan Cost = \$4.99 × 12 = \$59.88 per year
Web site maintenance cost = \$500 × 12 = \$6,000 per year

Initial investment = Server purchase cost + web site set up cost + SSL cost

On-going Operating cost = Utility cost + Rental Cost + Backup Cost + Server Maintenance & Upgrade + Virus Scan Cost + Web site maintenance cost + SSL Cost

First year operating cost = \$197.10 + \$240 + \$260 + \$50 + \$59.88 + \$6000 + \$69.99=\$6,876.97

For the 5th year, SSL certificate needs to be purchased at the end of the fourth year. Hence, SSL certificate cost will not be included in the end of 5th year cost.

Year	Cost category	Cost
0	Initial Investment	\$8,069.99
1	Operating cost	\$6,876.97
2	Operating cost	\$6,896.68
3	Operating cost	\$6,918.36
4	Operating cost	\$6,942.21
5	Operating cost	\$6,898.45

Table 12.3: Expenses associated with a server hosting a website

NPV of the 6 cash flows or TCO = \$34,244.40

The server purchase cost can be capitalized over 5 years. Server will be depreciated over 5 years. Initial web site set up cost can be capitalized for 5 years. The initial software development cost can be amortized over 5 years. Remaining portion of the initial investment will be treated as operating expense. Yearly operating cost will be treated as operating expense.

Example 12.4: Server is not purchased, but a virtual server is rented
Now, let's expand example 8.3 and consider that the server used to host a web site is not purchased and a virtual server is rented on a monthly basis which costs \$50 per month paid a year in advance. Business Compass LLC does not pay utility fee or rack space to place the server. Business Compass

LLC purchased a Linux Server to host its web site. The server needs to be running 24x7. The life of the server is 5 years. Assume that the borrowing cost to Business Compass LLC is 10% per annum. The server needs to be backed up once a week that costs $5 for backup. Server maintenance patches and other upgrades cost $50 on average for the life of the asset.

Linux-Apache-MySQL-PHP (LAMP) stack is used for hosting the web site. The web-site domain name is financeforitmanagegerssimplified.com. It costs $15.99 to purchase and renew the domain each year. The web site needs to be virus scanned daily. $4.99 is spent monthly to scan virus. Since the web site processes payment, the site needs a SSL certificate that costs $69.99 per year. SSL needs to be purchased at the beginning of the year.

The cost to develop the web site is $5000. Each month $500 is spent in maintenance and enhancement of the web site.

For simplicity, monthly costs are converted to annual cost and then, NPV is calculated. For finer granularity, APR can be converted to monthly interest rate by diving 12 and NPV can be calculated using monthly interest rate and monthly cost.

Server Hosting cost per annum is $50 per month $\times$ 12 months = $600 per year
Backup cost per year = $5 $\times$ 52 weeks= $260 per year
Virus Scan Cost = $4.99 $\times$ 12 = $59.88 per year
Web site maintenance cost = $500 $\times$ 12 = $6000 per year

Initial investment = One year hosting fee + Web site set up cost + SSL cost
= $600 + $5,000 + $69.99 = $5,669.99

On-going Operating cost = Server Hosting Cost + Backup Cost + Server Maintenance & Upgrade + Virus Scan Cost + Web site maintenance cost + SSL Cost

First year operating cost = $600 + $50 + $59.88 + $6000 + $69.99=$6,876.97

For the 5th year, SSL certificate and server hosting need to be purchased at the end of the fourth year. Hence, SSL certificate cost and server hosting cost will not be included in the end of 5th year cost.

Year	Cost category	Cost
0	Initial Investment	$5,669.99

Year	Cost category	Cost
1	Operating cost	$6,779.87
2	Operating cost	$6,779.87
3	Operating cost	$6,779.87
4	Operating cost	$6,779.87
5	Operating cost	$6,109.88

Table 12.3: Expenses associated with a server running LAMP stack

NPV of the 6 cash flows or TCO = $30,955.02

Example 12.5: TCO of ERP System

Business Compass® LLC's business started growing. To scale up its operation, it decided to purchase a world-class ERP package. The ERP package has three tiers – application tier, middleware-tier and database tier. Leading database is required to run the ERP package. The application, middleware and database tiers need to run on mid-range UNIX servers. Interfaces needed to be built to the existing customer support and CRM applications. ERP system offered pre-build reporting and analytics capability.

Assumptions:

1. It takes a year to implement the system.
2. Life of the system is 5 years after go-live.
3. The cost of capital is 10%.
4. All the license and maintenance fees are paid up front.

Cost components are as follows.

1. ERP package license costs $1,500,000 for 6 years.
2. Annual ERP Software Maintenance & Support Cost is 15% of purchase price.
3. Cost to implement the ERP system is $4,000,000.
4. To support the system, $1,000,000 in labor is spent annual after go-live.
5. Database license cost $100,000 for 6 years
6. Maintenance & Support cost of database is 15% of the license cost paid to the vendor
7. Mid-range server costs $400,000 to purchase. Three servers are required to support the ERP package.
8. Maintenance & Support cost of mid-range server 15% of the license cost paid to the mid-range server vendor
9. Cost to build the interfaces is $300,000.

10. The same staff that maintains the ERP package maintains interface. No additional money is spent on the maintenance of interface.
11. Cost of hosting 3 servers in data center is $50,000 per year
12. Network cost is $40,000 per year.

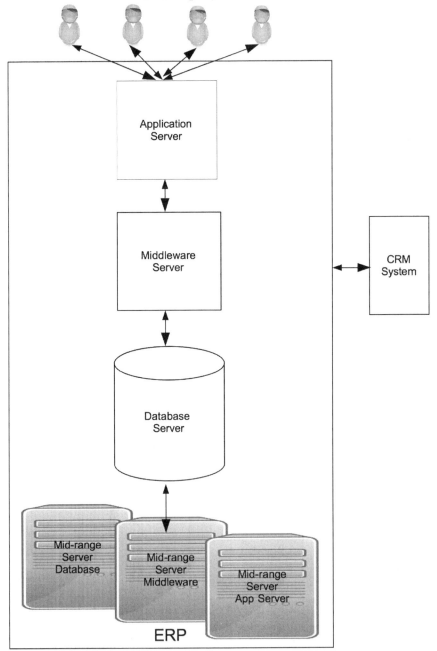

Figure 12.1: A logical ERP system diagram

Year	Cost category	Cost
0	ERP Package License	$1,500,000
0	ERP Maintenance Cost	$1,500,000 × 15% = $225,000
0	ERP Implementation Cost	$4,000,000
0	Cost to build interfaces	$300,000
0	Database License Cost	$100,000
0	Database Maintenance Cost	$100,000 × 15% = $15,000
0	Mid-range server cost of 3 servers	3 × $400,000 = $1,200,000
0	Mid-range server maintenance cost of 3 servers	$3 × $400,000 × 15% = $1,200,000× 15% = $180,000
0	Hosting cost	$50,000
0	Network Cost	$40,000
0	Total Cost	$7,610,000
1	ERP Maintenance Cost	$1,500,000 × 15% = $225,000
1	Database Maintenance Cost	$100,000 × 15% = $15,000
1	Mid-range server maintenance cost of 3 servers	$3 × $400,000 × 15% = $1,200,000× 15% = $180,000
1	Hosting cost	$50,000
1	Network Cost	$40,000
1	Labor cost to maintain the ERP System	$1,000,000
1	Total	$1,510,000
2	Total	$1,510,000
3	Total	$1,510,000
4	Total	$1,510,000
5	Total	$1,510,000

Table 12.4: Expenses associated with an ERP system

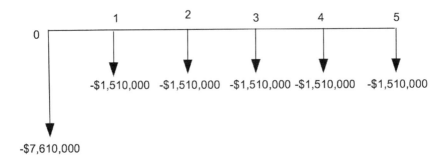

Figure 12.2: Cash (out)flow associated with an ERP system

NPV of the 6 cash flows = $7,610,000
+ $1,510,000× (1+10%)$^{-1}$ + $1,510,000 × (1+10%)$^{-2}$ + $1,510,000 × (1+10%)$^{-3}$ + $1,510,000 × (1+10%)-4 + $1,510,000 × (1+10%)$^{-5}$= $13,334,088

The TCO of the ERP system is $13,334,088.

Example 12.5: TCO of Data Warehousing System

Business Compass® LLC's business started growing. It needs effective ways to manage operational metrics and need to run what-if analysis. To meet this requirement, CFO of the company sponsored a Data Warehousing System project. This system will extract data from ERP, Customer Service and traffic from web, call centers and retail stores. Management wants to clean customer data and to merge US Postal Service Change of Address data so that audience lists generated for direct mail marketing receives least delivery issues due to bad address.

The data warehousing system requires an Extraction, Transformation Loading (ETL) tool to extract data from source systems and to load data to the data warehouse database. A large database license is required to store the data. Analytics. Database, Analytics and ETL each require a mid-range UNIX server of its own. Data Cleansing and ETL can be installed on the same server. Three mid-range UNIX servers are required to run database, analytics and ETL/Data Cleansing software.

Assumptions:

1. It takes a year to implement the system.

2. Life of the system is 5 years after go-live.
3. The cost of capital is 10%.
4. All the license and maintenance fees are paid up front.

Cost components are as follows.

1. ETL package license costs $100,000 per year.
2. Annual ETL Software Maintenance & Support Cost is 15% of purchase price.
3. Data cleansing package license costs $80,000 per year.
4. Annual Data Cleansing Software Maintenance & Support Cost is 15% of purchase price.
5. Analytics package license costs $60,000 per year.
6. Annual Analytics Software Maintenance & Support Cost is 15% of purchase price.
7. Database license cost $100,000 per year
8. Maintenance & Support cost of database is 15% of the license cost paid to the vendor
9. Mid-range server costs $400,000 to purchase. Three servers are required to support the Data Warehouse System.
10. Maintenance & Support cost of mid-range server 15% of the license cost paid to the mid-range server vendor
11. Cost of hosting 3 servers in data center is $50,000 per year
12. Network cost is $40,000 per year.
13. Cost to build the data warehousing system is $500,000.
14. Labor cost to maintain the system after go-live is $100,000 per year

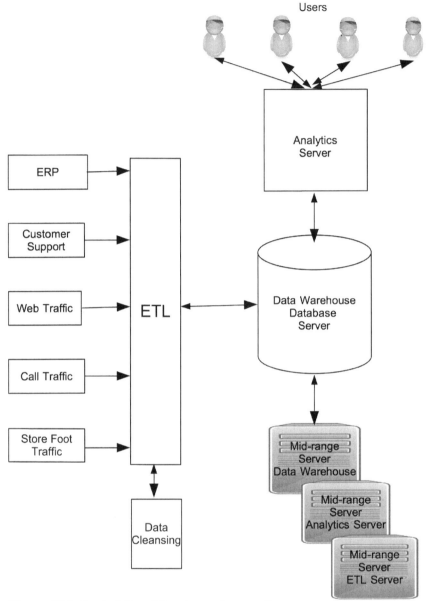

Figure 12.3: Logical Data Warehouse System diagram

Year	Cost category	Cost
0	ETL Package License	$100,000
0	ETL Maintenance Cost	$100,000 × 15% = $15,000
0	Data Cleansing Package	$80,000

Year	Cost category	Cost
	License	
0	Data Cleansing Maintenance Cost	$80,000 × 15% = $12,000
0	Analytics Package License	$60,000
0	Analytics Maintenance Cost	$60,000 × 15% = $9,000
0	Database License Cost	$100,000
0	Database Maintenance Cost	$100,000 × 15% = $15,000
0	Mid-range server cost of 3 servers	3 × $400,000 = $1,200,000
0	Mid-range server maintenance cost of 3 servers	$3 × $400,000 × 15% = $1,200,000× 15% = $180,000
0	Hosting cost	$50,000
0	Network Cost	$40,000
0	Cost to build the data warehousing system	$500,000
0	Total Cost	$2,361,000
1	ETL Maintenance Cost	$100,000 × 15% = $15,000
1	Data Cleansing Maintenance Cost	$80,000 × 15% = $12,000
1	Analytics Maintenance Cost	$60,000 × 15% = $9,000
1	Database Maintenance Cost	$100,000 × 15% = $15,000
1	Mid-range server maintenance cost of 3 servers	$3 × $400,000 × 15% = $1,200,000× 15% = $180,000
1	Hosting cost	$50,000
1	Network Cost	$40,000
1	Labor cost to maintain the Data Warehouse System	$100,000
1	Total	$421,000
2	Total	$421,000
3	Total	$421,000
4	Total	$421,000
5	Total	$421,000

Table 12.5: Expenses associated with a Data Warehouse System

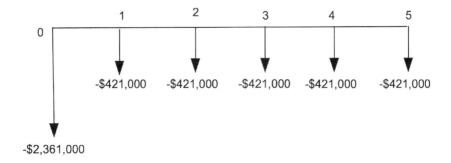

Figure 12.4: Cash (out)flow associated with a Data Warehouse System

NPV of the 6 cash flows = $2,361,000 + $421,000 × $(1+10\%)^{-1}$ + $421,000 × $(1+10\%)^{-2}$ + $421,000 × $(1+10\%)^{-3}$ + $421,000 × $(1+10\%)^{-4}$ + $421,000 × $(1+10\%)^{-5}$= $3,956,921

The TCO of the Data Warehousing system is $ 3,956,921

Example 12.6: TCO of a Mobile App

Business Compass® LLC decided to launch a mobile app named MBA Sidekick. This app has great potential to capture the MBA student and finance professional segment. CTO decided to launch the application on all the three major mobile app platforms. Development team will release on all the platforms at the same time for the first time. Then, each two months, the development team will release a release for each platform resulting in 6 releases per year. Business Compass® LLC plans to keep the app on the markets for 3 years. Cost of capital is 10%.

The SDK to develop mobile app for major platform is available for $999 per platform per year paid up front. The development team consists of 3 developers, an architecture and a tester who salary is $100,000, $130,000 and $80,000 per annum respectively. Initial release will take 6 months of time. After that every 2 months team will publish a new release on each platform.

Development team will receive 5% salary raise every year.

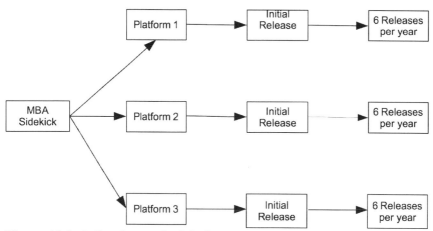

Figure 12.5: Agile release schedule for MBA Sidekick mobile app

Initial Development Cost = 3 × $100,000 × 6/12 + $130,000 × 6/12 + $80,000 × 6/12 = $150,000 + $65,000 + $40,000 = $255,000 or $255,000 ÷ 6 monthly.

First 3 bi-monthly releases = 3 × $100,000 × 2/12 + $130,000 × 2/12 + $80,000 × 2/12 = $25,000 + $21,666.66 + $13,333.33 = $60,000 or $30,000 monthly.

Second 6 bi-monthly release = $60,000 × (1+5%) = $63,000 or $31,500 monthly.

Third 6 bi-monthly release = $63,000 × (1+5%) = $66,150 or $33,075 monthly.

Forth 3 bi-monthly release = $66,150 × (1+5%) = $69,457 or $34,728.50 monthly.

End of Month	Year	Release	Cost category	Cost
6	0	0	Initial Development Cost	$255,000
8	0	1	Release	$60,000
10	0	2	Release	$60,000
12	0	3	Release	$60,000
14	1	4	Release	$63,000
16	1	5	Release	$63,000
18	1	6	Release	$63,000
20	1	7	Release	$63,000

End of Month	Year	Release	Cost category	Cost
22	1	8	Release	$63,000
24	1	9	Release	$66,150
26	2	10	Release	$66,150
28	2	11	Release	$66,150
30	2	12	Release	$66,150
32	2	13	Release	$66,150
34	2	14	Release	**$66,150**
36	2	15	Release	$66,150
38	3	16	Release	$69,457
40	3	17	Release	$69,457
42	3	18	Release	$69,457

Table 12.6: Per release cost

Monthly cost and present value

Month	Salary Cost	Present Value
1	$42,500	$42,148.76
2	$10,000	$9,835.39
3	$10,000	$9,754.11
4	$10,000	$9,673.50
5	$10,500	$10,073.23
6	$10,500	$9,989.98
7	$30,000	$28,306.90
8	$30,000	$28,072.96
9	$30,000	$27,840.96
10	$30,000	$27,610.86
11	$30,000	$27,382.68
12	$30,000	$27,156.37
13	$31,500	$28,278.54
14	$31,500	$28,044.83
15	$31,500	$27,813.05
16	$31,500	$27,583.19
17	$31,500	$27,355.23
18	$31,500	$27,129.16
19	$31,500	$26,904.95
20	$31,500	$26,682.60

Month	Salary Cost	Present Value
21	$31,500	$26,462.08
22	$31,500	$26,243.38
23	$31,500	$26,026.50
24	$31,500	$25,811.40
25	$33,075	$26,877.99
26	$33,075	$26,655.86
27	$33,075	$26,435.56
28	$33,075	$26,217.08
29	$33,075	$26,000.41
30	$33,075	$25,785.53
31	$33,075	$25,572.43
32	$33,075	$25,361.09
33	$33,075	$25,151.49
34	$33,075	$24,943.63
35	$33,075	$24,737.48
36	$33,075	$24,533.04
37	$34,728.50	$25,546.62
38	$34,728.50	$25,335.49
39	$34,728.50	$25,126.11
40	$34,728.50	$24,918.45
41	$34,728.50	$24,712.51
42	$34,728.50	$24,508.28
Net Present Value		$1,040,599.67

Table 12.7: NPV of Salary

Year	SDK License Cost	Present Value
0	$999	$999
1	$999	$908.18
2	$999	$825.61
3	$999	$750.56
Net Present Value		$3,483.36

Table 12.7: NPV of SDK Cost

TCO = NPV of Development Cost + NPV Of SDK License Cost = $1,044,083.03

13 CHARGE BACK

Many IT projects create products and services that are internally used by various divisions of business and IT. Chargeback model allows recouping the cost against appropriate cost center or project. Use of private cloud, use of middleware hardware & software, load testing platform, use of analytics platform, use of ETL, use of mainframe are some of the examples where chargeback model is appropriate. This chapter will explain how to identify cost elements and how to translate the cost to a utility or chargeback model.

Type of systems for which chargeback model is used:

- Private Cloud
- Performance or Load or Stress Testing
- Reporting
- Shared Service
- Cloud
- Mainframe
- Architecture
- Web Service
- Helpdesk
- Asset Management

Typical costs associated are as follows:
- Part of the cost
- Hardware Purchase Cost
- Hardware Data Center Hosting Cost
- Software License Cost
- Hardware and Software Maintenance & Support cost
- Direct Labor involved with implementing and supporting
- Indirect Labor
- Service Provider Costs
- Hosting/Cloud Provider
- Overhead

First of all, the costs associated with system for which charge back model needs to be developed need to be identified. Secondly, the usage pattern – volume, timing when the system is used need to be estimated. Finally, a chargeback model can be developed.

Example 13.1 Load Testing CoE - Business Compass® LLC decided to build a Performance Testing Center of Excellence (CoE) to test the performance of the applications when the applications are released for the first time and before each major release subsequently. The CoE set up an environment to test up to 500 concurrent users. It purchased required hardware, software and virtual user license to ramp up load. It also formed a team to able to analyze the load requirement, design load scenario and develop load test scripts as well as execute the scripts, identify bottlenecks and recommend remedy to resolve the bottlenecks.

Cost elements:
1. A mid-range server to run the load testing engine. Purchase price is $200,000 and annual maintenance cost is 15% of purchase price.
2. Five Linux Servers to generate load. Purchase price is $2000 and maintenance is 15% per annum
3. Load test software will cost $50,000 and the annual maintenance fee is 15%
4. 500 perpetual virtual user generator license which costs $500 per license
5. A head of CoE at $120,000 salary per annum
6. A performance test architect at $100,000 salary per annum
7. Five load test scripters at $70,000 salary per annum
8. 20% of hardware + software cost is added for DBA, SA, Network Admin support
9. 15% of overall labor cost is attributed to management overhead

Assumptions:
1. Life of the system is 3 years
2. Cost of Capital is 10%
3. Maintenance fee goes up 10% a year
4. Employees receive 5% annual raise on average
5. Maintenance fee is paid to the vendors up-front for the year

Up front hardware and software cost =
Mid-range server purchase cost + Mid-range server purchase cost +
Linux server purchase cost + Linux server maintenance cost +
Load Testing Software cost + Load Testing Software Maintenance +

500 perpetual Load generator license cost
$=\$200,000 + \$200,000 \times 15\% + \$2000 \times 5 + \$2000 \times 5 \times 15\% +$
$\$50,000 + \$50,000 \times 15\% + 500 \times \$500$
$= \$549,000$

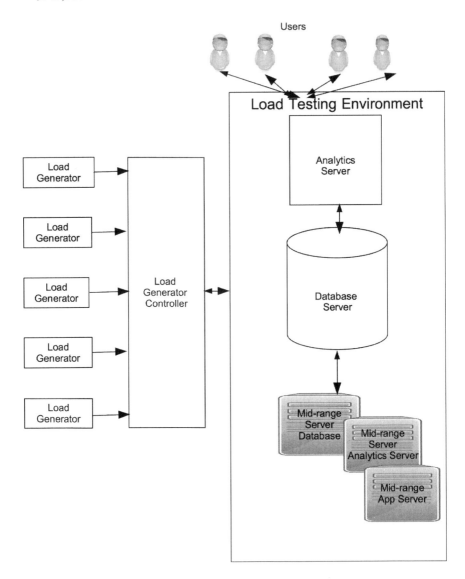

Figure 13.1: Load Testing System Logical Architecture Diagram

First year labor cost =
Salary of Head of CoE +
Salary of Head of CoE Performance Architect +

Salary of Head of CoE Load Test Scripts +
System Administration Cost +
Management Cost
=($120,000 + $100,000 + 3 × $70,000 + $549,000 × 20%) × (1+15%)
=$620,770

First year monthly labor cost =$647,174 ÷ 12 = $51,730

Second year hardware and software maintenance cost = First year
maintenance cost × (1+10%)
= $41,800

Second year labor cost = First Year Labor Cost × (1+5%) = $620,770 ×
(1+5%) = $651,808

Second year monthly labor cost $651,808 ÷ 12 = $54,317

Third year hardware and software maintenance cost = Second Year
maintenance Cost × (1+10%) = $45,980× (1+10%)
= $45,980

Third year labor cost = Second Year Labor Cost × (1+5%) = $651,808
× (1+5%) = $684,398

Third year monthly labor cost =$684,398 ÷ 12 = $57,033

Year	Cost category	Cost
0	Hardware and Software Purchase + 1 year Maintenance	$549,000
1	Second year hardware and software maintenance cost	$41,800
2	Third year hardware and software maintenance cost	$45,980

Table 13.1: Hardware & software purchase plus maintenance cost

NPV of Hardware and Software purchase and maintenance over 3 years
= $625,000

Month	Salary Cost	Present Value
1	$51,730	$51,302.48
2	$51,730	$50,878.49

Month	Salary Cost	Present Value
3	$51,730	$50,458.01
4	$51,730	$50,041.00
5	$51,730	$49,627.44
6	$51,730	$49,217.29
7	$51,730	$48,810.54
8	$51,730	$48,407.15
9	$51,730	$48,007.09
10	$51,730	$47,610.33
11	$51,730	$47,216.86
12	$51,730	$46,826.64
13	$54,317	$48,762.07
14	$54,317	$48,359.08
15	$54,317	$47,959.42
16	$54,317	$47,563.06
17	$54,317	$47,169.98
18	$54,317	$46,780.14
19	$54,317	$46,393.53
20	$54,317	$46,010.11
21	$54,317	$45,629.86
22	$54,317	$45,252.76
23	$54,317	$44,878.77
24	$54,317	$44,507.87
25	$57,033	$46,347.16
26	$57,033	$45,964.12
27	$57,033	$45,584.25
28	$57,033	$45,207.53
29	$57,033	$44,833.91
30	$57,033	$44,463.38
31	$57,033	$44,095.92
32	$57,033	$43,731.49
33	$57,033	$43,370.07

Month	Salary Cost	Present Value
34	$57,033	$43,011.64
35	$57,033	$42,656.17
36	$33,075	$24,533.04
Net Present Value		$1,661,468.64

Table 13.2: Monthly Salary and NPV

NPV of Hardware & Software + Labor = $625,000 + $1,661,468.64 = $2,286,468.64

Let's estimate the monthly cost, which is a payment.
PV = $2,286,468.64, rate = 10%÷12, term = 12 × 3 = 36 months

Monthly Payment = $73,7717.91

The chargeback should break-even the expense. The Load Testing CoE needs to charge back $73,7717.91.

The Load Testing CoE can be utilized for 16 hours a day 7 days a week and 365 days a year.

Per hour, the CoE needs to charge back $73,7717.91 ÷ (30 days/month *16 hours/day)= $153.70.

The charge back rate is $153.70 per hour.

Example 13.2 Incident Management System - Business Compass® LLC decided to implement an incident management tool to efficiently manage support issues. The incident management software cost $50,000. Support cost is 15% per annum. It costs $10,000 hardware to run the software. Six resources manage the software including maintenance. Incident management software needs to run 24x7. Average salary per resource is $50,000 per year. Let's calculate per hour charge back for using incident management system. Assume that the cost of capital is 10% and that there are no other costs associated. Software has a life of 3 years.

Initial cost = software purchase + maintenance + hardware = $50,000 + 15% × $50,000 + $10,000 = $67,500
First year labor = 6 × $50,000 = $300,000 or $25,000 per month
Second year maintenance payable at the end of the first year = $7,500
Second year labor = 6 × $50,000 = $300,000 or $25,000 per month
Third year maintenance payable at the end of the second year = $7,500

Third year labor = $300,000 or $25,000 per month

Year	Cost category	Cost
0	Hardware and Software Purchase + 1 year Maintenance	$67,500
1	Second software maintenance cost	$7,500
2	Third year software maintenance cost	$7,500

Table 13.3: Hardware & software purchase plus maintenance cost

NPV of Hardware and Software purchase as well as maintenance cost = $80,516.53

Month	Salary Cost	Present Value
1	$25,000	$51,302.48
2	$25,000	$50,878.49
3	$25,000	$50,458.01
4	$25,000	$50,041.00
5	$25,000	$49,627.44
6	$25,000	$49,217.29
7	$25,000	$48,810.54
8	$25,000	$48,407.15
9	$25,000	$48,007.09
10	$25,000	$47,610.33
11	$25,000	$47,216.86
12	$25,000	$46,826.64
13	$25,000	$48,762.07
14	$25,000	$48,359.08
15	$25,000	$47,959.42
16	$25,000	$47,563.06
17	$25,000	$47,169.98
18	$25,000	$46,780.14
19	$25,000	$46,393.53
20	$25,000	$46,010.11

Month	Salary Cost	Present Value
21	$25,000	$45,629.86
22	$25,000	$45,252.76
23	$25,000	$44,878.77
24	$25,000	$44,507.87
25	$25,000	$46,347.16
26	$25,000	$45,964.12
27	$25,000	$45,584.25
28	$25,000	$45,207.53
29	$25,000	$44,833.91
30	$25,000	$44,463.38
31	$25,000	$44,095.92
32	$25,000	$43,731.49
33	$25,000	$43,370.07
34	$25,000	$43,011.64
35	$25,000	$42,656.17
36	$25,000	$24,533.04
Net Present Value		$1,661,468.64

Table 13.4: Monthly salary and NPV of salary

NPV of hardware & software procurement, maintenance and labor = $1,480,297.42.

Estimated Monthly Cost

PV = $1,480,297.42.
Interest rate = 10%÷12 per month
Term = 36 months

Payment = $47,765.03

System runs 24×7.

So, hourly cost = $47,765.03 per month ÷ (30 days/month × 24 hours/day) = $66.34

Any project that will require incident management would need to pay $66.34.

If the aggregated hours the system to be used is known or can be estimated, then the charge back rate can be refined further.

Example 13.3 Private Cloud Business Compass® LLC decided to build a private cloud to be used by diverse teams within its IT department to ramp up software development. In order to build the private cloud, Business Compass® LLC leased a data center. It purchased 1,000 Linux servers with 4 CPUs and 16 GB RAM, 20 TB disk array, Virtualization Software, and Provisioning Software. It hired a team of 20 System Administrators, Network and Storage Engineers. The life of the system is 5 years. Cost of Capital is 10%.

Cost of Linux Server = $1000 per server
Cost of Maintenance Support is 15% of the purchase price
Cost of Disk Array = $300,000
Cost of Storage Maintenance Support is 15% of the purchase price
Cost of Virtualization Software is $300,000
Cost of Virtualization Software Maintenance is 15%
Cost of Provisioning Software is $100,000
Cost of Maintenance Support of provisioning software is 15%
Average Salary of Staff is $100,000 per year
Data Center Lease Costs $50,000 per month paid up front
Maintenance Fee on license is paid in advance

Initial hardware and software purchase & maintenance cost =
Server Purchase Price +
Server maintenance support cost +
Disk Array purchase cost +
Disk Array maintenance support cost +
Virtualization software purchase cost +
Virtualization software maintenance cost +
Provisioning software purchase cost +
Provisioning software annual maintenance cost +
First month data center lease payment =
1000×$1000 + 1000×$1000 ×15% + $300,000 + $300,000 × 15% +
$300,000 + $300,000 × 15% + $100,000 + $100,000 × 15% + $50,000
= $2,005,000

Subsequent Annual hardware & software maintenance support cost =
Server maintenance support cost +
Disk Array maintenance support cost +
Virtualization software maintenance cost +
Provisioning software annual maintenance cost = $255,000

Monthly cost = Salary + Data Center Lease Cost = \$50,000 + \$100,000 × 20 = \$2,050,000

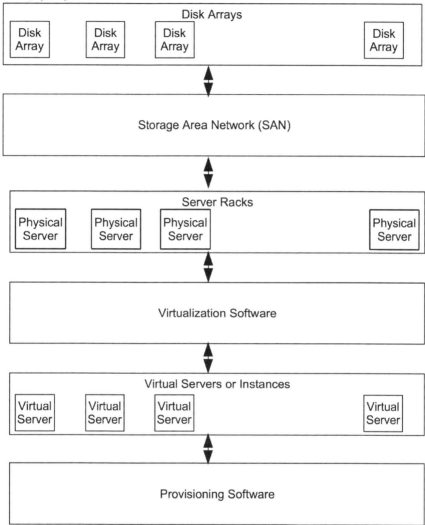

Figure 13.2: Logical Virtual Private Cloud Architecture Diagram

Year	Cost category	Cost
0	Initial hardware and software purchase & maintenance cost	\$2,005,000
1	Subsequent Annual hardware & software maintenance support cost	\$255,000

Year	Cost category	Cost
2	Subsequent Annual hardware & software maintenance support cost	$255,000
3	Subsequent Annual hardware & software maintenance support cost	$255,000
4	Subsequent Annual hardware & software maintenance support cost	$255,000

Table 13.5: Hardware and software purchase plus maintenance cost

NPV of Hardware and Software purchase as well as annual maintenance cost paid in advance = $2,813,315.69

NPV of Server + Maintenance = $1,260,945.29

NPV of Storage + Maintenance = $378,283.59

NPV of Software + Maintenance = $504,378.12

Month	Salary Cost	Present Value
1	$216,667	$214,876.03
2	$216,667	$213,100.20
3	$216,667	$211,339.04
4	$216,667	$209,592.44
5	$216,667	$207,860.27
6	$216,667	$206,142.41
7	$216,667	$204,438.76
8	$216,667	$202,749.18
9	$216,667	$201,073.57
10	$216,667	$199,411.80
11	$216,667	$197,763.77
12	$216,667	$196,129.36
13	$216,667	$194,508.46
14	$216,667	$192,900.95
15	$216,667	$191,306.73

16	$216,667	$189,725.68
17	$216,667	$188,157.70
18	$216,667	$186,602.67
19	$216,667	$185,060.50
20	$216,667	$183,531.08
21	$216,667	$182,014.29
22	$216,667	$180,510.04
23	$216,667	$179,018.22
24	$216,667	$177,538.73
25	$216,667	$176,071.47
26	$216,667	$174,616.34
27	$216,667	$173,173.23
28	$216,667	$171,742.04
29	$216,667	$170,322.69
30	$216,667	$168,915.06
31	$216,667	$167,519.07
32	$216,667	$166,134.61
33	$216,667	$164,761.60
34	$216,667	$163,399.93
35	$216,667	$162,049.52
36	$216,667	$160,710.27
37	$216,667	$159,382.09
38	$216,667	$158,064.88
39	$216,667	$156,758.56
40	$216,667	$155,463.03
41	$216,667	$154,178.21
42	$216,667	$152,904.01
43	$216,667	$151,640.34
44	$216,667	$150,387.12
45	$216,667	$149,144.25
46	$216,667	$147,911.65
47	$216,667	$146,689.24

48	$216,667	$145,476.93
49	$216,667	$144,274.64
50	$216,667	$143,082.29
51	$216,667	$141,899.79
52	$216,667	$140,727.07
53	$216,667	$139,564.03
54	$216,667	$138,410.61
55	$216,667	$137,266.72
56	$216,667	$136,132.29
57	$216,667	$135,007.23
58	$216,667	$133,891.47
59	$216,667	$132,784.92
60	$216,667	$131,687.53
Net Present Value		$10,197,496.62

Table 13.6: Monthly salary and NPV of Salary

NPV of labor and lease cost = $10,197,496.62

NPV of labor cost = $7,844,228.17

NPV of data center lease = $2,372,879.02

Sum total NPV of hardware, software, maintenance cost, labor and lease cost or TCO = = $10,197,496.62+ $2,813,315.69 = $ 13,010,812.31

Payment of PV $ 13,010,812.31 at 10% ÷ 12 monthly interest rate over 5 years (60 months) = $276,441.31

Cost per hour = $276,441.31 ÷ (30 days/month × 24 hours/day) = $38.39 per hour of utilization

NPV of Server + Maintenance = $1,260,945.29

NPV of Storage + Maintenance = $378,283.59
NPV of Software + Maintenance = $504,378.12
NPV of data center lease = $2,372,879.02
NPV of labor cost = $7,844,228.17

Let's say, 4 instances can be created on each physical server with 1 CPU and 4 GB of RAM per instance.

	Server	Storage	Software	Lease	Labor
NPV	$1,260,945.29	$378,283.59	$504,378.12	$2,372,879.02	$7,844,228.17
Monthly Cost	$26,791.36	$8,037.41	$10,716.54	$50,416.67	$166,666.67
Resources					20
Servers	1000		1000	1000	1000
Instances per server	4		4	4	4
Total instances	4000		4000	4000	4000
Hours per month	720	720	720	720	4800
Hourly Cost Per Server	$37.21		$14.88	$70.02	$34.72
Per Instance Cost Per Hour	$0.0093		$0.0037	$0.0175	$0.0087
Disk Storage in GB		20480			
Hourly Cost of Disk		$11.16			
Hourly Cost per GB of Disk		$0.0005			

Table 13.7: Unit cost

A way to calculate the hourly cost of virtual server request

0.0093 I + 0.0005 D + 0.0037 + 0.0175 + 0.0887 =
0.0093 I + 0.0005 D + 0.1099

where I is number of 1 CPU 4 GB RAM instances and D is per GB disk

Labor, lease and software cost per instance per hour is fixed.

14 FINANCING VS. LEASING

From an economic sense, it is beneficial to the firms to translate fixed cost to variable cost. Leasing offers in such avenue. The cost benefit of leasing can be compared to purchasing equipment. Depending on the cost of lease vs. cost of purchase, the asset can be purchased or leased.

Lease payment consists of depreciation fee, finance fee and sales tax in some states. Some states charge sales tax up front. Some states charge sales tax on down payment. Some states charge sales tax on monthly lease payment. Taxation for lease varies by state.

Depreciation fee = (Net Capitalized Cost − Residual Value) ÷ Lease Term in Months.

Finance Fee = (Net Capitalized Cost + Residual Value) × Money Factor

Money Factor = APR ÷ 2400

Money factor is a constant factor that is used to determine average interest rate on a loan. When a loan is amortized, the interest paid decreases and the principal paid is increased over the term. But, for a lease payment, the interest paid remains the same for each period within the loan term. Therefore, APR divided by 2400 instead of 1200 to arrive at money factor.

Capitalized Cost = Negotiated purchase price + Taxes & fees − Down Payment

Lease Payment = (Depreciation Fee + Finance Fee) × (1+Sales Tax %)

Lease Payment

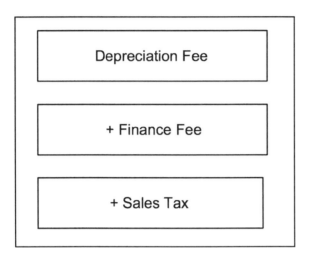

Figure 14.1: Lease Payment

Cost of Lease = Total lease payment + up-front costs + Down payment

Cost of Purchase = Monthly loan payments over the lease term + Down payment – Market Value at the end of the lease term

Example 14.1: Business Compass® LLC is considering acquiring a new mid-range server for $2,000,000. It has two options – (b) to borrow at 5% for 5 years from the vendor's financing arm, (b) to lease the equipment from the same vendor at 6%. The residual value of the equipment is 10% of the purchase price. Assume that the state where Business Compass® LLC and the equipment vendor is located does not charge sales tax. There are no other up front cost or end of lease cost.

Net Capitalized Cost = $2,000,000
Residual Value = $2,000,000 ×10% = $200,000
Depreciation = Net Capitalized Cost – Residual Value = $2,000,000-$200,000 = $1,800,000
Term = 5 years = 5 years × 12 months/year = 60 months
Depreciation Fee = $1,800,000÷60=$30,000
Money Factor = 6 ÷ 2400 = 0.0025
Finance Fee = (Net Capitalized Cost + Residual Value) × Money Factor = ($1,800,000 + $200,000) × 0.0025 = $2,000,000 × 0.0025 = $5,000
Lease Payment = (Depreciation Fee + Finance Fee) × (1+Sales Tax %) = $30,000+$5,000 = $35,000

Monthly Loan Payment = $37,742

Cost of Lease = Total lease payment + up-front costs + Down payment
= $35,000 × 60 = $2,100,000

Cost of Purchase = Monthly loan payments over the lease term + Down payment – Market Value at the end of the lease term
= $37,742× 60 - $200,000
= $2,264,548 - $200,000 = $2,064,548

Let's assume the Market Value at the end of the lease term is the residual value, which is $200,000.

In this case, the option to purchase the equipment through financing is economically superior to the option to lease.

Example 14.2: Business Compass® LLC is considering acquiring a new mid-range server for $2,000,000. It has two options – (b) to borrow at 5% for 5 years from the vendor's financing arm, (b) to lease the equipment from the same vendor at 6%. The residual value of the equipment is 10% of the purchase price. Assume that the state where Business Compass LLC and the equipment vendor are located requires 7% sales tax to be charged. Sales tax is charged on lease payments, but not collected up front. However, for purchases, sales tax is charged up front. There are no other up front cost or end of lease cost.

Net Capitalized Cost = $2,000,000
Residual Value = $2,000,000 ×10% = $200,000
Depreciation = Net Capitalized Cost – Residual Value = $2,000,000-$200,000 = $1,800,000
Term = 5 years = 5 years × 12 months/year = 60 months
Depreciation Fee = $1,800,000÷60=$30,000
Money Factor = 6 ÷ 2400 = 0.0025
Finance Fee = (Net Capitalized Cost + Residual Value) × Money Factor
= ($1,800,000 + $200,000) × 0.0025 = $2,000,000 × 0.0025 = $5,000
Lease Payment = (Depreciation Fee + Finance Fee) × (1+Sales Tax %)
= ($30,000+$5,000) × (1+7%) = $35,000 × 1.07=$37,450

For loan payment, the loan amount is $2,000,000 × (1+7%) = $2,140,000
Monthly Loan Payment = $40,384.44

Cost of Lease = Total lease payment + up-front costs + Down payment
= $35,000 × 60 = $2,100,000

Let's assume the Market Value at the end of the lease term is the residual value, which is $200,000.

Cost of Purchase = Monthly loan payments over the lease term + Down payment – Market Value at the end of the lease term
= $40,384.44× 60 - $200,000
= $2,423,066.40 - $200,000 = $2,223,066.40

In this case, the option to lease is economically superior to to purchase the equipment through financing.

Example 14.2: Business Compass® LLC is considering acquiring a new mid-range server for $2,000,000. It has two options – (b) to borrow at 5% for 5 years from the vendor's financing arm, (b) to lease the equipment from the same vendor at 6%. The residual value of the equipment is 10% of the purchase price. Assume that the state where Business Compass LLC and the equipment vendor are located requires 7% sales tax to be charged. Sales tax is charged up front both on lease and on purchases. Sales tax is not charged on monthly lease payments. There are no other up front cost or end of lease cost.

Net Capitalized Cost = $2,000,000 × (1+7%) = $2,140,000
Residual Value = $2,000,000 ×10% = $200,000
Depreciation = Net Capitalized Cost – Residual Value = $2,140,000
-$200,000 = $1,940,000
Term = 5 years = 5 years × 12 months/year = 60 months
Depreciation Fee = $1,940,000÷60=$32,333.33
Money Factor = 6 ÷ 2400 = 0.0025
Finance Fee = (Net Capitalized Cost + Residual Value) × Money Factor
= ($2,140,000 + $200,000) × 0.0025 = ($2,340,000 × 0.0025 = $5,850

Sales tax is not charged on monthly lease payments, but charged up front.

Lease Payment =
(Depreciation Fee + Finance Fee) =
$32,333.33 + $5,850 = $38,183.33

For loan payment, the loan amount is $2,000,000 × (1+7%) = $2,140,000
Monthly Loan Payment = $40,384.44

Cost of Lease = Total lease payment + up-front costs + Down payment
= $38,183 × 60 = $2,291,000

Let's assume the Market Value at the end of the lease term is the residual value, which is $200,000.

Cost of Purchase = Monthly loan payments over the lease term + Down payment – Market Value at the end of the lease term
$$= \$40,384.44 \times 60 - \$200,000$$
$$= \$2,423,066.40 - \$200,000 = \$2,223,066.40$$

In this case, the option to purchase through financing is economically superior to lease the equipment.

Lease can be treated as capital lease or as operating lease for accounting purpose. In case, the lease is treated as capital lease, the leased asset is depreciated. In case the lease is treated as operating lease, the lease payment is expensed. These two different treatments affects bottom line. A lease that satisfies one of the 4 conditions (acronym SNOB) is treated as a capital lease; otherwise, the lease is treated as operating lease.

S – Lease life exceeds 75% of the asset life

N – NPV of the lease payments exceeds 90% of asset value

O – Ownership transfer to the lessee at the end of the lease

B – Option to purchase at a "bargain price" at the end of the lease

Whether lease is economically superior depends on the lease terms and the competing options. However, it offers a way to translate fixed cost to variable cost.

15 COST BENEFIT ANALYSIS

Cost benefit analysis is a way to weigh money spent against revenue generated or benefits earned or cost reduced. This is a way to compare projects or investments. This allows making sound investment decision. Cost can be expressed as a series of cash outflows. Benefit can be expressed as a series of cash in flows. By taking the out and in flows, the NPV of the series of cash flows can be generated discounting by the cost of the capital for the subject company. If the NPV is positive, the project should be pursued. Among competing projects the project with highest NPV is the winner. Similarly, IRR can be generated from the cash flows. If the IRR of the project is higher than the cost of capital, then the project is economically profitable. Among competing projects, the project with highest IRR is the winner. In case of two or more projects produce the same IRR, then the NPV of each project needs to be weighed and one with highest NPV wins.

Example 15.1 Business Compass® LLC decided to diversify from mobile and financial apps to global distribution system (GDS) to consolidate hotel, airline, rental car inventory and offer data to hotels, airlines and rental car companies to present the inventory to the customers to make a reservation. Business Compass® LLC earns a fee for each reservation.

Three mid-range servers to host database, application server and search engine. Each server costs $150,000 to purchase and incurs 15% annual maintenance fee paid in advance.

Database license costs $50,000 per year and incurs 15% annual maintenance fee paid in advance

Middle-ware license costs $100,000 per year and incus 15% annual maintenance fee paid in advance

Business Compass® LLC is estimated to spend $1,000,000 to develop the system. It will take a year to develop the system. Then, on an annual basis, it would spend $300,000 to maintain the system.

Business Compass® LLC will earn revenue from the commission on the reservations made using its GDS engine as follows.

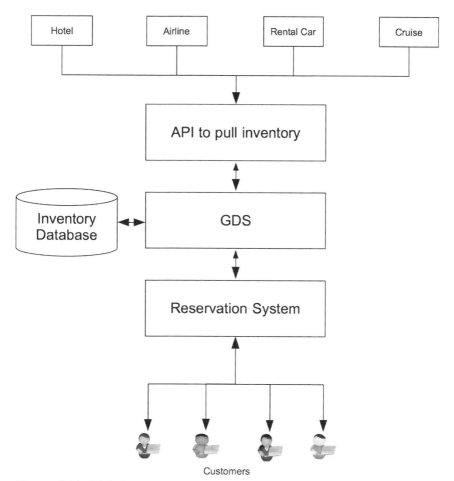

Figure 15.1: Global Distribution System Logical Architecture Diagram

MM = Million	Hotel	Airline	Car Rental	Cruise	Vacation Package
Monthly average bookings	1900	3995	6000	1000	2320
Commis sion	$7	$20	$8	$50	$90
Monthly Commis sion	$13,300	$79,90 0	$48,000	$50,000	$0.208MM

Total Monthly Commission					$0.04MM
Yearly Commission	$159,600	$958,800	$576,000	$600,000	$2.5MM
Total Yearly Commission					$4.8MM

Table 15.1: Revenue stream

Month	Cost Category	Expense	Revenue	Gross Profit = Revenue – Expense
0	Mid-range server cost	$450,000		$(450,000)
0	Mid-range server maintenance	$67,500		
0	Database License	$50,000		
0	Database License Maintenance Fee	$7,500		
0	Middleware License	$100,000		
0	Middleware license maintenance fee	$15,000		
1	Development Cost	$83,333		$(83,333)
2	Development Cost	$83,333		$(83,333)
3	Development Cost	$83,333		$(83,333)
4	Development Cost	$83,333		$(83,333)
5	Development Cost	$83,333		$(83,333)
6	Development Cost	$83,333		$(83,333)
7	Development Cost	$83,333		$(83,333)

Month	Cost Category	Expense	Revenue	Gross Profit = Revenue – Expense
8	Development Cost	$83,333		$(83,333)
9	Development Cost	$83,333		$(83,333)
10	Development Cost	$83,333		$(83,333)
11	Development Cost	$83,333		$(83,333)
12	Development Cost	$83,333		$(173,333)
12	Mid-range server maintenance	$67,500		
12	Database License Maintenance Fee	$7,500		
12	Middleware license maintenance fee	$15,000		
13	Maintenance cost	$25,000	$400,000	$375,000
14	Maintenance cost	$25,000	$400,000	$375,000
15	Maintenance cost	$25,000	$400,000	$375,000
16	Maintenance cost	$25,000	$400,000	$375,000
17	Maintenance cost	$25,000	$400,000	$375,000
18	Maintenance cost	$25,000	$400,000	$375,000
19	Maintenance cost	$25,000	$400,000	$375,000
20	Maintenance cost	$25,000	$400,000	$375,000
21	Maintenance cost	$25,000	$400,000	$375,000
22	Maintenance cost	$25,000	$400,000	$375,000
23	Maintenance cost	$25,000	$400,000	$375,000
24	Maintenance cost			$285,000

Month	Cost Category	Expense	Revenue	Gross Profit = Revenue − Expense
		$25,000	$400,000	
24	Mid-range server maintenance	$67,500		
24	Database License Maintenance Fee	$7,500		
24	Middleware license maintenance fee	$15,000		
25	Maintenance cost	$25,000	$400,000	$375,000
26	Maintenance cost	$25,000	$400,000	$375,000
27	Maintenance cost	$25,000	$400,000	$375,000
28	Maintenance cost	$25,000	$400,000	$375,000
29	Maintenance cost	$25,000	$400,000	$375,000
30	Maintenance cost	$25,000	$400,000	$375,000
31	Maintenance cost	$25,000	$400,000	$375,000
32	Maintenance cost	$25,000	$400,000	$375,000
33	Maintenance cost	$25,000	$400,000	$375,000
34	Maintenance cost	$25,000	$400,000	$375,000
35	Maintenance cost	$25,000	$400,000	$375,000
36	Maintenance cost	$25,000	$400,000	$285,000
36	Mid-range server maintenance	$67,500		
36	Database License Maintenance Fee	$7,500		
36	Middleware license maintenance fee	$15,000		

Month	Cost Category	Expense	Revenue	Gross Profit = Revenue − Expense
37	Maintenance cost	$25,000	$400,000	$375,000
38	Maintenance cost	$25,000	$400,000	$375,000
39	Maintenance cost	$25,000	$400,000	$375,000
40	Maintenance cost	$25,000	$400,000	$375,000
41	Maintenance cost	$25,000	$400,000	$375,000
42	Maintenance cost	$25,000	$400,000	$375,000
43	Maintenance cost	$25,000	$400,000	$375,000
44	Maintenance cost	$25,000	$400,000	$375,000
45	Maintenance cost	$25,000	$400,000	$375,000
46	Maintenance cost	$25,000	$400,000	$375,000
47	Maintenance cost	$25,000	$400,000	$375,000
48	Maintenance cost	$25,000	$400,000	$285,000
48	Mid-range server maintenance	$67,500		
48	Database License Maintenance Fee	$7,500		
48	Middleware license maintenance fee	$15,000		
49	Maintenance cost	$25,000	$400,000	$375,000
50	Maintenance cost	$25,000	$400,000	$375,000
51	Maintenance cost	$25,000	$400,000	$375,000
52	Maintenance cost	$25,000	$400,000	$375,000
53	Maintenance cost			$375,000

Month	Cost Category	Expense	Revenue	Gross Profit = Revenue – Expense
		$25,000	$400,000	
54	Maintenance cost	$25,000	$400,000	$375,000
55	Maintenance cost	$25,000	$400,000	$375,000
56	Maintenance cost	$25,000	$400,000	$375,000
57	Maintenance cost	$25,000	$400,000	$375,000
58	Maintenance cost	$25,000	$400,000	$375,000
59	Maintenance cost	$25,000	$400,000	$375,000
60	Maintenance cost	$25,000	$400,000	$375,000
			NPV	$11,703,796
			IRR	10.65%

Table 15.2: Monthly revenue, expense, gross profit, NPV and IRR

NPV of the cash flows is positive. IRR 10.65% is greater than cost of capital 10%. Therefore, Business Compass® LLC should pursue the project.

How to decide winning project?

- NPV > 0 for a project
- Highest NPV among multiple projects
- IRR > Cost of Capital in case of lending which is the case with IT projects
- IRR < Cost of Capital in case of borrowing
- Highest IRR among multiple projects
- If IRR of two or more projects is the same, use NPV to decide

16 OFF-SHORING & OUTSOURCING

Companies contract non-core IT work to vendors. Vendors can be located on-site, off-site or offshore. Similarly, companies create captive IT companies and relocate work offshore. Companies do so for scalability, business continuity, 24x7 coverage and cost efficiency. A vendor performs outsourcing. Whatever the rationale for off shoring or outsourcing maybe, cost efficiency is a core decision criteria. Often times, outsourcing offers a means to translate fixed cost to variable cost.

The decision criterion for outsourcing and off shoring is as follows.

- Achieving Cost Efficiency
- Converting fix cost to variable cost
- Productivity Gain
- Core vs. Non-Core
- Protecting Intellectual Property
- Availability of talent
- Build Business Continuity
- Achieve Scale
- Follow the sun Coverage
- Cost of retention

If maintaining intellectual property is key concern, then off shoring to captive IT may be superior to outsourcing to a vendor. Cost efficiency has been a predominant factor to decide whether to offshore through captive IT or a vendor.

Example 16. Business Compass® LLC needed to speed up the development of mobile app. It required 30 mobile app developers. Business Compass LLC could not locate the resources in its home city of Randolph,

New Jersey. So, it explored the options to hire. Luckily, it was able to locate the resources in Bhubaneshwar, Odisha, India that is a hub for large IT companies. Let's go through a series of hypothetical scenarios to understand the intricacies of outsourcing.

	USA	India
Programmer hourly	$70	$25
Payroll Tax	12.50%	
Benefits	7%	15%
Raise	5%	15%
Cost per hour	$88	$33

Table 16.1: On-site vs. Off-shore cost comparison

Dollar for dollar Business Compass benefits economically.

Let's assume that since Bhubaneshwar is an IT hub, the resources are subject to switching jobs fast. Resources need to be retained constantly. This reduces the productivity to 70% in Bhubaneshwar. Also, assume that the productivity of US resource is 90%. Now, the cost per hour increases on both sides, but in Bhubaneshwar in higher proportion.

	USA	India
Programmer hourly	$70	$25
Payroll Tax	12.50%	
Benefits	7%	15%
Raise	5%	15%
Cost per hour	$88	$33
Productivity	90%	60%
Cost after factoring productivity	$98.31	$55.10

Table 16.2: On-site vs. Off-shore cost comparison with productivity factor

Let's consider an external factor – exchange rate fluctuation. A new government came to power in India in May 2014. The government took a series of steps to curb the fall of Indian Rupee (INR). Due to that the INR appreciated 15%.

	USA	India
Programmer hourly	$70	$25
Payroll Tax	12.50%	

Benefits	7%	15%
Raise	5%	15%
Cost per hour	$88	$33
Productivity	90%	60%
Cost after factoring productivity	$98.31	$55.10
Currency Appreciation		15%
After factoring currency appreciation	$98.31	$64.83

Table 16.1: On-site vs. Off-shore cost comparison with currency fluctuation

Since, the payroll expense in India amounted to $50,000,000, CFO of Business Compass decided to hedge INR fluctuation by purchasing foreign currency swap. However, due to new crisis arising in the Middle East, INR weakened against US Dollar. Therefore, the premium paid for purchasing foreign currency swap was lost. This raised the cost per hour even higher.

There are many factors that need to be considered to make an off-shoring or outsourcing decision. Cost efficiency is a key factor, but there are other ones.

17 BUSINESS CASES

Business Case is a document that captured a problem, recommended solution, cost to build the solution and the benefits received from the solution. The benefits are quantified and cost benefit analysis prepared. As part of the business case, NPV and IRR analysis is carried out. If the NPV is positive then project is suitable to be carried out. If a project from multiple projects needs to be selected, then the project with highest NPV wins. From IRR point of view, the IRR of the project needs to be higher than the cost of capital. If multiple projects are compared, then the one with highest IRR wins. If two or more projects yield the same IRR, then the project with highest NPV wins. This chapter will focus on the financial aspects of the business case.

First of all, the cost components need to be identified. Next, the revenue components need to be identified. Then, 3 to 5 year cost and revenue projection need to be performed. NPV of the net cash flow using company's cost of capital need to be calculated. Similarly, using the cash flows, IRR needs to be calculated.

Costs associated with IT applications are as follows.
- Hardware Purchase
- Hardware Maintenance Cost
- Cost to host the hardware
- Public IP Address Cost
- Domain Cost
- SSL Cost
- Internet cost for bandwidth
- Software License Cost
- Software License Maintenance

- Labor cost to customize software
- Labor cost to maintain application
- Labor cost to administer hardware
- Labor cost from employee salary
- Labor cost from vendors
- SaaS or PaaS cost
- Helpdesk Support Cost

IT projects are carried out to increase revenue, reduce cost, build efficiency, satisfy legal, compliance or regulatory requirements or to build competitive advantage. Depending on the project the cost and revenue

Type	Example	Business Drivers
Generate Revenue	<ul><li>Web Order Management</li><li>ERP</li><li>Marketing Campaign Management</li><li>CRM</li></ul>	<ul><li>Increase order volume</li><li>Reduce order processing time</li><li>Single call resolution</li><li>Increase per order revenue</li></ul>
Reduce Cost	<ul><li>Outsource</li><li>Offshore</li><li>Virtualization</li><li>Private Cloud</li><li>Shared Services</li><li>Open Source</li></ul>	<ul><li>Reduce labor cost</li><li>Reduce hardware cost</li><li>Reduce shared service cost</li><li>Reduce licensing cost</li></ul>
Building competitive advantage	<ul><li>Outsource</li><li>Offshore</li><li>Virtualization</li><li>Private Cloud</li><li>Build CoE</li><li>Data Warehousing</li><li>Analytics</li></ul>	<ul><li>Build scale</li><li>Build business continuity</li><li>Build round the sun coverage</li><li>Gain insights to sell more</li><li>Reduce attrition</li></ul>
Optimization & Productivity Gain	<ul><li>Virtualization</li><li>Private Cloud</li><li>Shared Services</li></ul>	<ul><li>Reduce to time required to create an environment</li></ul>

Type	Example	Business Drivers
Compliance, Legal, Regulatory	• Export Compliance • Anti-Money Laundering • Know Your Customer (KYC) • Basel II Requirements • Sarbanes-Oxley (SOX) compliance	• Prevent shipping to a country under embargo • Prevent money laundering • Prevent fraud • Maintain required Tier 1, 2 and 3 capital ratios • Satisfy SEC independence requirements

Table 17.1: Type of IT Projects

Example 17.1: Business Compass® LLC decided to make airplane games. Each game is shipped with predetermined sets of airplane models. Other airplane models can be purchased through in-app purchase. Development team will take a year to build the games and models. Equity investors funded the product development, sales and marketing.

Let's first consider the sales volume.

	Year				
Revenue	1	2	3	4	5
Number of airplane mobile app games	0	1	1	2	4
Volume					
Plane models per airplane mobile app games	0	5,000	50,000	100,000	100,000
Plane models	0	5,000	50,000	200,000	400,000
Bundle of game and airplane models	0	1	3	3	3
Games and sets of airplane models	0	5,000	150,000	600,000	1,200,000
Bundles of games and sets airplane models paid for	0	0	100,000	400,000	800,000
Average unit price per airplane model	$45	$45	$45	$45	$45
Average unit price per game and airplane models	15	15	15	15	15
Average production cost per airplane model	30	30	20	20	20
Average production cost per game and airplane model sets	5	5	3	3	3
Discount	100%	100%	0%	0%	0%

Table 17.2: Sales volume.

Next, consider the income statement - revenue, expense, and free cash flow. Free Cash Flow (FCF) is the cash flow available to equity investors after all the other payment have been made.

Income Statement		1	2	3	4	5
Sales Revenue						
Sales revenue from Plane models		0	0	2,250,000	9,000,000	18,000,000
Sales Revenue from game and patches		0	0	1,500,000	6,000,000	12,000,000
Gross Sales revenue from game and patches		**0**	**0**	**3,750,000**	**15,000,000**	**30,000,000**
Less returns and defects	5%	0	0	187,500	750,000	1,500,000
Less cost of warranty	10%	0	0	375,000	1,500,000	3,000,000
Net Sales Revenue		**0**	**0**	**3,187,500**	**12,750,000**	**25,500,000**
Cost of Goods Sold (% of Sales Revenue)		0	25,030	1,450,000	5,800,000	11,600,000
Gross Profit		**0**	**(25,030)**	**1,737,500**	**6,950,000**	**13,900,000**
Gross Profit Margin %				46%	46%	46%
Industry Gross Profit Margin %		38%	38%	38%	38%	38%
Expenses						
R&D	5%	35,000	10,000	250,000	250,000	350,000
Advertisement	10%	0	50,000	200,000	250,000	250,000
SG&A	20%	0	150,000	500,000	750,000	1,000,000
Total		35,000	210,000	950,000	1,250,000	1,600,000
Operating Income or EBITDA		**(35,000)**	**(235,030)**	**787,500**	**5,700,000**	**12,300,000**
Depreciation & Amortization	0%	0	0	0	0	0
EBIT		(35,000)	(235,030)	787,500	5,700,000	12,300,000
Interest Expense	10%	0	0	(63,420)	(63,420)	(63,420)
Pre-Tax Income		(35,000)	(235,030)	850,920	5,763,420	12,363,420
Tax	35%	0	0	297,822	2,017,197	4,327,197
Net Income		(35,000)	(235,030)	553,098	3,746,223	8,036,223
Free Cash Flow		1	2	3	4	5
Net Income		(35,000)	(235,030)	553,098	3,746,223	8,036,223
Interest Expense		0	0	(63,420)	(63,420)	(63,420)
(1-T) x Interest Expense		0	0	(41,223)	(41,223)	(41,223)
Depreciation & Amortization		0	0	0	0	0
Working Capital	24%	0	0	900,000	3,600,000	7,200,000
CapEx						
FCF		(35,000)	(235,030)	(388,125)	105,000	795,000

Income Statement		1	2	3	4	5
IRR	14%					
Debt		(120,000)	(240,000)	(225,000)	(634,200)	(634,200)
Interest Expense	10%	(12,000)	(37,200)	(63,420)	(63,420)	(63,420)
Total Debt		(132,000)	(409,200)	(634,200)	(697,620)	(697,620)
Breakeven Year	3					
Breakeven Quantity	11,627					

Table 17.2: Income statement

From IRR analysis, the project will generate 14% IRR. This will break even in 3 years and the volume required to break even is 11,627.

An example of a revenue generating IT project is presented below. This was presented in chapter 15.

In summary, the criterion to decide a winning project is as follows.

- NPV > 0 for a project
- Highest NPV among multiple projects
- IRR > Cost of Capital in case of lending which is the case with IT projects
- IRR < Cost of Capital in case of borrowing
- Highest IRR among multiple projects
- If IRR of two or more projects is the same, use NPV to decide

ABOUT THE AUTHOR

Sribatsa Das holds a Bachelors and Masters in Computer Science. He holds an MBA from New York University's Leonard N. Stern School of Business in Finance and Strategy. Sribatsa's passion is technology. He strives at bringing technological innovative products to life every day leveraging his long technology career and finance education. Sribatsa started as a DBA and application developer in his early career. After 20+ years long stint in IT and consulting, he embarked upon entrepreneurship. He launched Business Compass® LLC mobile app start-up venture in 2008. This start-up has launched 200+ mobile apps. MBA Sidekick, Mobile Statistics Professor® and Altman Z-Score+ are his key innovations. MBA Sidekick offers a full array of analytical tools to MBA students and professionals. MBA Statistics Professor provides tools to carry out college and MBA level statistical analysis. Altman Z-Score+ analyzes credit risk of companies worldwide including bond rating equivalent and up to 10 years of default probability. This product is available on leading financial data terminal via APPS ALTMAN <GO> command. Business Compass LLC's web sites are http://businesscompassllc.com and http://altmanzscoreplus.com. More details about this book including templates can be found at http://financeforitmanagers.com.

17812572R00058

Made in the USA
San Bernardino, CA
18 December 2014